**EVEREST** **1067**

A Collection of Contemporary Turkish Literature

# ORHAN KEMAL

Orhan Kemal – the pen name of Mehmet Raşit Öğütçü – is one of Turkey's best-loved writers. He was born in Adana in 1914. His father became a Member of Parliament in the first session of the Turkish National Assembly and founded the Popular Party in 1930. The consequences of his political activities led the family to emigrate to Syria and Lebanon, leaving their son unable to complete his secondary education. These events are covered in Orhan Kemal's semi-autobiographical novel *My Father's House* (1949), which he referred to as the 'diaries of a nobody'. He was later to return to the town of his birth and worked in a variety of jobs in cotton factories and as a clerk at the Foundation for the Eradication of Tuberculosis. This period of his life, including his marriage to the daughter of a Yugoslav immigrant in 1937, was to become the subject of four future novels.

During his military service in 1939 he was sentenced to five years' imprisonment for his political views. Time spent with the celebrated writer Nâzım Hikmet in the Bursa State Prison had an important influence on Kemal's socialist political stance, and these are described in his memoirs of this period.

He moved to Istanbul in 1951, where he started to write full time. His works often centre on ordinary people struggling to make a living. Inspired initially by his own experiences in the 1920s and 1930s, he went on to explore such themes as the problems of farm and factory workers, the alienation of migrant workers in big cities, the lives of prison inmates, blind devotion to duty, child poverty and the repression and exploitation of women.

He was the author of thirty-eight works of fiction, comprising twenty-eight novels and ten collections of stories, several of which have been filmed or turned into plays. He died in Sofia, Bulgaria, in 1970 and is buried in Istanbul.

# IN JAIL WITH NÂZIM HİKMET

## Orhan Kemal

Translation and Introduction by
Bengisu Rona

§

Publication No. **1067**

Contemporary Turkish Literature **16**

**In Jail With Nâzım Hikmet**
Orhan Kemal

Original Title:
*Nâzım Hikmet'le 3.5 Yıl*

Translated by Bengisu Rona
Cover Design by Utku Lomlu
Page Layout by M. Atahan Sıralar

First English Edition: April 2012

ISBN: 978 - 605 - 141 - 009 - 8
Certifacate No: 10905

Printed by Melisa Matbaacılık
Printery Certifacate No: 12088
Tel: +90 (0212) 674 97 23
Fax: +90 (0212) 674 97 29

EVEREST PUBLICATIONS
Ticarethane Sokak No: 53 Cağaloğlu/ISTANBUL
Tel: +90 (212) 513 34 20-21 Fax: +90 (212) 512 33 76
Distribution: Alfa, Tel: +90 (212) 511 53 03 Fax: +90 (212) 519 33 00
e-mail: info@everestyayinlari.com
www.everestyayinlari.com
www.twitter.com/everestkitap

Everest is a trademark of the Alfa Publishing Group

# Contents

# GUIDE TO TURKISH PRONUNCIATION

Current spelling convention of Modern Turkish is used through-out. The pronunciation of the letters is roughly similar to the equivalent characters in English. Letters not found in English and those pronounced differently from English are given below:

c pronounced like the 'j' in 'jam'

ç pronounced like the 'ch'in 'church'

ğ no distinct pronunciation, but it lengthens the preceding vowel

ı pronounced much like the 'er' in 'letter' or 'speaker'

ö similar to the vowel sound in 'dirt'

ş pronounced like the 'sh' in 'ash'

ü pronounced like the French 'tu' or the German city 'Lübeck'

A circumflex accent indicates that the vowel is lengthened and sometimes that the preceding sound is palatalised.

# TRANSLATOR'S NOTE AND ACKNOWLEDGEMENTS

※

The idea for this book emerged from my teaching twentieth-century Turkish Literature at the School of Oriental and African Studies, University of London. The way politics shaped the literary canon and the extent to which the literary works reflected political developments in Turkey were a central theme in those classes. Nowhere is this more evident than in the writings of two people: Nâzım Hikmet in poetry and Orhan Kemal in prose.

Published and planned translations of Orhan Kemal's novels also made me think it was the appropriate time to present to the English-speaking readers another work, which is not a novel and does not speak about the lives of the vivid characters of Orhan Kemal, but rather reveals a particular period in the lives of the author himself and of Nâzım Hikmet. Orhan Kemal's prison memoirs *Nâzım Hikmet'le 3,5 Yıl* (*Three and a Half Years with Nâzım Hikmet*) illustrate the bond which developed between the two men and show how the older poet inspired the young man to move away from trying to become a poet and to concentrate on developing as a novelist.

The poems of Orhan Kemal presented here have not been previously translated, and although some of Nâzım Hikmet's poems included in the memoirs have been translated earlier, I chose to provide new translations for these as well. I am grateful to my colleagues and friends for their suggestions on a number of translation points. Natasha and George Lemos have been very generous with their time, reading through the translated text and making extremely helpful comments. I would also like to thank successive years of postgraduate students with whom I charted the progression of Turkish literature and whose responses informed me. I am grateful to Işık Öğütçü, Orhan Kemal's youngest son, and to the Orhan Kemal Museum for making the documents in their archives available to me and always being ready to answer my questions.

# INTRODUCTION

Orhan Kemal's mid-to-late twenties were blighted by a harsh prison sentence, but ironically this was also the making of him as a writer.

His reminiscences describe how the friendship between the two developed from the moment Nâzım Hikmet arrived at Bursa Prison, and they offer a unique insight into Orhan's development as a writer, as well as Nâzım's inspiration for his most celebrated poem *Human Landscapes from my Country*. Throughout their time together in jail, Orhan Kemal, with Nâzım's approval, made copious notes on him, detailing his moods, his thoughts, his feelings and even his gestures. He was hoping to publish these at a later date, but unfortunately most of the notes were lost. Those that did survive were collected, along with some of the letters Nâzım had sent Orhan Kemal from prison after his release in September 1943, and are published here alongside Orhan's recollections. Nâzım was to remain in Bursa Prison for almost another seven years after Orhan left.

Nâzım had been held in a succession of prisons in Ankara and Istanbul, including one particularly harsh period on board the naval vessels *Yavuz* and *Erkin*. In August 1938, he was taken to Sultanahmet Prison in Istanbul, where he shared a cell with Kemal Tahir, who was to become one of Turkey's leading novelists and one of Nâzım Hikmet's closest friends. Kemal Tahir (1910–1973), like Nâzım, had been arrested and jailed in 1938 for allegedly instigating mutiny in the navy. He was sentenced to 15 years; Nâzım received a 28-year sentence. The two were later transferred to Çankırı Prison in Central Anatolia, north of Ankara, where the winters were severe. Nâzım applied for a transfer to the spa town of Bursa, which was nearer Istanbul and had a milder climate. He was moved there in December 1940.

Nâzım's time in Bursa Prison was critical to the composition of *Human Landscapes from my Country*, not least because it brought him into contact with an extraordinary range of people from very different backgrounds, whose life stories he realised were a critical element in the emergence of modern Turkey from the wreckage of the defeated Ottoman Empire. The epic incorporates a section about the Turkish War of Independence, as well as an account of Hitler's invasion of the Soviet Union and the response of the Soviet Army. Verses about the fighting itself are interspersed with scenes where prisoners are following the progress of the war as they listen to short-wave radio broadcasts in a Turkish jail. Orhan Kemal's reminiscences provide a unique insight into an extraordinary, deprived and squalid environment which shaped and inspired *Human Landscapes from my Country*, introducing us to many of the real individuals who appeared as characters in this epic.

As is clear from the charge sheet which led to his imprisonment and, as he himself acknowledges, Orhan Kemal had been a fan of Nâzım Hikmet long before they actually met in person. He knew many of the poems by heart and, in *Three and a Half Years with Nâzım Hikmet*, he expects his readers to be familiar with the poet's work too, and to recognise the quotations and allusions.

When he first hears that Nâzım is coming to Bursa, Orhan recalls and quotes short extracts from five of his best-known

6

poems. The first two date from the early twenties. 'Orchestra' ('*Orkestra*') was written around the time Nâzım Hikmet first joined the Communist Party, while 'Mechanisation' ('*Makinalaşmak İstiyorum*') was written in Moscow in 1923, in praise of the technological advances of the period. The third poem quoted is 'The Caspian Sea' ('*Hazer Denizi*'). Nâzım first saw the Caspian in 1922 during a long journey from Batum on the Black Sea Coast to Moscow: the train went via Baku in Azerbaijan. But the poem was written in Moscow in 1928, during his second visit to the Soviet Union. The poem describes the boat's Turcoman helmsman sitting cross-legged like a statue of Buddha, wearing a huge black sheepskin cap reminiscent of an unshorn sheep cut open at the belly. A few pages later, Orhan remembers these details as he waits to see Nâzım after his arrival at Bursa Prison. He is expecting someone like the marble figure of the poem: the reality turns out to be very different.

The fourth poem quoted by Orhan Kemal is 'Answer' ('*Cevap*'). This was written in 1929: Nâzım had returned from Moscow the preceding year and had spent six months in jail on his arrival. He used the poem again in 1932 within a longer composition, 'Why did Benerci kill himself ?' ('*Benerci kendini niçin öldürdü?*'), about Banerjee, a revolutionary student refugee from British-ruled India whom he had met in Moscow in the early twenties.

The final poem quoted by Orhan Kemal in this opening section of the book is 'The Fifth Letter to Taranta-Babu' ('*Taranta-Babu'ya Beşinci Mektup*'), written in 1935 in protest to Mussolini's invasion of Abyssinia. The poem is presented as letters written by an Ethiopian student in Italy to his wife Taranta-Babu in Ethiopia. This allowed Nâzım to attack the brutality of the fascists while avoiding censorship by the Turkish authorities, who had banned criticism of Italian foreign policy.[1]

---

1    Göksu and Timms 1999, p. 123.

Two other poems are quoted by Orhan Kemal later in the book. 'They' (*'Onlar'*) is the opening section of 'The National Forces' (*'Kuvâyi Milliye'*), an epic depicting the key events of the Turkish War of Independence from the end of the First World War up until the final victory over the invading Greek army in 1922. 'The Eyes of the Starving' (*'Açların Gözbebekleri'*) was written in 1922, just after Nâzım Hikmet arrived in Moscow for the first time, shocked by the scenes of starving people he had seen in the famine areas he had travelled through during his journey there.

Orhan Kemal also refers to two other poems just by their titles. One is 'The Epic of Sheikh Bedrettin, Son of the Kadi of Simavna' (*'Simavne Kadısı oğlu Şeyh Bedrettin destanı'*). Written in 1936, it is the story of a fifteenth-century Islamic scholar who led a movement to share all property after Anatolia had been devastated by war. The movement was suppressed, and the sheikh hanged. 'La Gioconda' (*'Jokont'*), written in 1929, is a dialogue between a young Chinese revolutionary whom Nâzım met in Moscow in the early 1920s and the portrait of the Mona Lisa in the Louvre. The two fall in love and the Mona Lisa follows the young man to China, where she sees him executed before she returns to France where she is tried and burnt at the stake.[1]

Orhan Kemal also illustrates how Nâzım works, describing him jumping out of bed in the middle of the night during a gale and frantically writing a couple of lines on the cell wall before going back to sleep. These two lines were to form part of the first verse of the poem 'Southerly Gale' (*'Lodos'*).

Orhan Kemal and Nâzım Hikmet: Writers on Trial

Orhan Kemal and Nâzım Hikmet came to Bursa Prison from very different backgrounds, but the circumstances of their ar-

---

1   Göksu and Timms 1999, p. 90.

rests and trials were not dissimilar. Both were arrested and tried in military courts. The 36-year-old Nâzım was convicted in 1938, firstly of inciting mutiny in the army and secondly (in a separate trial) of inciting mutiny in the navy; Orhan, who had just started his military service in 1938 following the birth of his first daughter Yıldız (who features in Nâzım's letters), was convicted of producing propaganda on behalf of a foreign state and inciting mutiny. He served almost his full sentence of five years. Nâzım, seen by the authorities as a much more serious threat and sentenced to 28 years, was not released until an amnesty in 1950.

Orhan Kemal had been denounced by fellow soldiers. A book by Maxim Gorky, along with some newspaper cuttings about Marxist ideas and poems he had addressed to Nâzım Hikmet, had been found among his belongings. Nâzım Hikmet, a committed Marxist, had been arrested along with a group of cadets at the Military Academy in Ankara. The cadets had been reading left-wing books and discussing Marxism, and one of them had called on Nâzım Hikmet twice, presumably because he admired him. Nâzım was suspicious and told him to go away, complaining to the chief of police, thinking the cadet was an informer seeking to entrap him. In fact, the cadet was himself denounced by one of his fellows and was tried along with the poet. Nâzım's second trial involved alleged left-wing activities among young men in the navy who met to discuss literature. There was no evidence that Nâzım had had any contact with naval personnel, but he was accused of inciting a potential revolt.[1]

These trials coincided with the international uncertainty in the run-up to the Second World War and took place during the last months of Mustafa Kemal Atatürk's life, when he was gravely ill and the leading figures in the Republic were position-

---

1    Ibid, p. 155. They provide a detailed account of both the army and navy trials on pp. 138–158.

ing themselves for the succession. The severity of the sentences and the extent to which Marxist thinking in general, and Nâzım Hikmet in particular, were seen as a threat in Turkey in the late thirties, particularly within the Armed Forces, can only be fully understood within the context of the history of communist activity in Turkey since the First World War and of relations between the young Turkish Republic and its northeastern neighbour, the Soviet Union.

For most of the nineteenth and early twentieth centuries, Tsarist Russia had been a major threat to Turkey. Istanbul and parts of Anatolia had periodically been overrun by waves of Muslim refugees from the Balkans, the Crimea and the Caucasus who had fled progressive Russian advances and the independence struggles of the Serbs, Greeks and Bulgarians.

In the aftermath of the First World War, however, both the Bolsheviks and the Turkish nationalists were struggling for survival. Neither could afford a re-run of the Russian–Turkish wars or of the First World War campaigns on Turkey's eastern front. Both faced an immediate threat from the Allied powers. Turkey, which had been fighting almost continuously since the start of the Balkan Wars in 1912, was in 1919 faced with the invasion of southern Anatolia by the Italians, and of İzmir and the Aegean coast by the Greeks. French troops had already occupied the region around Adana. Istanbul was not formally occupied until March 1920, but in reality Allied forces had been in charge of the city since the 1918 armistice.

In these circumstances it was natural for the nationalists in Anatolia and the Bolsheviks in Moscow to look to each other for support. By mid-1919, the nationalists in Ankara were discussing the possibility of a tactical alliance with the Bolsheviks. Mustafa Kemal[1] argued that Turkey should be neutral in the conflict between the Bolsheviks and the Allied powers, but that

---

1    Mustafa Kemal took the surname Atatürk in 1934 – see note on p. 209

contact should be established immediately with Moscow to see whether they could supply arms, ammunition, equipment, money and, 'if necessary', men.[1] He regarded the newly independent republics of Armenia, Georgia and Azerbaijan as a possible threat, as they could be used by the British to attack the Turkish nationalist forces from the east. He also saw them as a physical obstacle to the potential supply of arms and ammunition from the Bolsheviks.[2]

In April 1920, after the formal occupation of Istanbul in March, the Turkish Grand National Assembly convened in Ankara.[3] On April 26, two days after he was elected President of the Assembly, Mustafa Kemal sent a telegram to Moscow agreeing to cooperate with the Bolsheviks 'in their effort to save the oppressed from imperialist governments'.[4] He offered to help them in the Caucasus in exchange for gold, ammunition, equipment and supplies.

That same day, the Red Army entered Azerbaijan and two days later took control of the Republic. In May, the Turkish Grand National Assembly sent its Foreign Minister to Moscow, and the Turkish leadership turned its attention to the Armenian Republic, which was occupying Kars. Kars fell to the Turks on October 30, 1920, and in December the Bolsheviks took over the government of Armenia.

Meanwhile in Istanbul, the Ottoman government had signed the Treaty of Sèvres on August 10, 1920, which was intended to

---

1    Mango 1999, p. 232.
2    Hale 2000, p. 50.
3    Its members had originally been elected in late autumn 1919 as members of the Chamber of Deputies of the Ottoman Empire.
     The Chamber, dominated by nationalists, assembled in Istanbul in January 1920, but after the occupation a number of them were exiled by the British to Malta. The Sultan formally dissolved the Chamber, and the remaining members made their way to Ankara, where they reconvened as the Turkish Grand National Assembly.
4    Mango 1999, p. 278.

put an end to the war between the Ottoman Empire and the victorious powers.[1] But it was never accepted by the Turkish Grand National Assembly in Ankara, nor was it ever implemented. Turkey had no other sources of potential support, and Moscow now became a natural ally. On March 16, 1921, a Treaty of Friendship was signed in Moscow.

The young Nâzım Hikmet was still in Istanbul at the beginning of the occupation. But fellow writers were already in Ankara, and in November 1920, he and Vala Nurettin, a fellow poet and friend, received an invitation to join them. The two finally left the Ottoman capital on January 1st, 1921. They travelled by boat along the Black Sea coast to the port of İnebolu, where they had to obtain travel permits to continue to Ankara. The town was full of people waiting for their permits, and they met a number of Turkish students who had been involved in the German Spartacus revolt – an abortive leftwing uprising in Berlin in 1919 – and had subsequently been deported to Turkey. Those two weeks in İnebolu provided the two poets with their introduction to communist ideology.[2] The permits for Nâzım Hikmet and Vala Nurettin eventually arrived, and they started on the arduous two-week trek over the mountains to Ankara.

Another arrival in Ankara was the new Soviet Consul, and the consulate became a centre for various radical groups. Marxist ideas were circulating among the young nationalists, and parallels were being drawn between their struggle for survival and that of the Bolsheviks.[3] With the Treaty of Friendship signed, it was not surprising that communist sympathisers started to emerge and make themselves heard.

---

1   The treaty outraged many Turks, as it carved out large areas of the territory claimed by the Turkish nationalists and awarded them to Greece and Italy, while creating an independent Armenia enlarged to include Erzurum and Trabzon.
2   Göksu and Timms 1999, p. 17.
3   Ibid, p. 21.

While Mustafa Kemal was eager to obtain practical Soviet support for the national cause, he was well aware of the dangers posed to his leadership by communist revolutionaries operating on the ground outside Ankara, across Anatolia. With Baku now under Soviet control, the Turkish Communist Party held its Congress there in September 1920. Messages were sent to Ankara indicating support for the nationalist struggle, but the party was at the same time working to establish a network of supporters inside Turkey. The Congress made it clear that cooperation with the nationalists was only a temporary expedient; the real target was to work towards a seizure of power by the working class.[1]

Mustafa Kemal had also been concerned by the emergence of a secret political organisation known as the Green Army in the spring of 1920. It was a large, amorphous group apparently committed to radical socialist thinking within an Islamic context. It had supporters in the Assembly, but was particularly strong in the Eskişehir region, which was under the control of the Circassian Ethem, commander of one of the major nationalist irregular units. Ethem had been a strong supporter of Enver Paşa and the Committee of Union and Progress (*İttihat ve Terakki Cemiyeti*), the organisation behind the 1908 revolution which had controlled the government during the First World War, many of whose followers (particularly the Circassians) had been impressed by Lenin's commitment to liberate the subject nationalities of the Tsarist Empire and had, for that reason, embraced communist thinking.[2] Eskişehir became a centre of Marxist thought and press activity.

Mustafa Kemal was alarmed. He had already forced the resignation of a newly elected interior minister[3] he believed to have

---

1 Harris 1967, p. 64
2 Mango 1999, p. 291.
3 In this pre-Republican period in Ankara, ministers were elected by the Turkish Grand National Assembly.

been a communist agent, and he feared that the chairman of the Turkish Communist Party in Baku, Mustafa Suphi, had agents who were working to foment a pro-Soviet revolution in Turkey. In September 1920, the Treason Law was extended to include political as well as military subversion, and in October Mustafa Kemal instructed a group of his followers to set up an official Turkish Communist Party. All legal communist activity would now take place within this party. It was hoped this would allow the nationalist movement to exploit the energies of radical Marxists and enable the government to move against Moscow-backed communists within Turkey without appearing to be anti-communist.

This official party caused considerable confusion among communists in Anatolia, particularly when it was announced that the Green Army was being taken over by the official Turkish Communist Party. The Turkish Army then moved against Ethem, who was defeated in early January 1921. He himself fled and joined the invading Greek forces.

At this point, Mustafa Suphi, chairman of the Turkish Communist Party based in Baku, decided to move to Turkey. He went initially to Kars, where he stayed for some weeks and met Kâzım (Karabekir) Paşa. On January 28, Suphi embarked from Trabzon on a boat provided by the harbour master, Yahya Kemal, who was a close supporter of Enver Paşa. Suphi and his party were all killed in circumstances which remain obscure. Whether Yahya was acting on his own initiative in seeking revenge against Suphi as a possible rival to Enver, or whether he was acting under instructions from Ankara is unclear. But the murder eliminated the possibility of the pro-Moscow Communist Party becoming a threat to Ankara in the immediate future, and Turkish communists – not least Nâzım Hikmet – certainly blamed Ankara.

This incident appears to have been formative in Nâzım's political development, although he did not learn about the murders for another eight months. He subsequently wrote a poem,

14

'For the Fifteen' ('*Onbeşler için*'), and a verse play '28 January' ('*28 Kânunisani*'), about the assassination.

He and Vala Nurettin had expected to be enlisted in the nationalist forces after they arrived in Ankara. This, however, did not happen, and in April 1921 they were sent as teachers to the small town of Bolu, west of Ankara. They stayed there until September, discussing literature and politics with like-minded friends in their spare time, before deciding to make their way to the port of Batum (Batumi) in Soviet-controlled Georgia. They took a boat to Trabzon and got themselves posted as teachers to Kars, arguing that to get there they needed to go via Batum. This enabled them to obtain a permit to cross the frontier. It was while they were in Trabzon that they learnt what had happened to Mustafa Suphi and his companions.[1] They went on to Batum, which was where they became members of the Turkish Communist Party. The following year they took the train to Moscow, passing the scenes which inspired the poem 'The Eyes of the Starving' ('*Açların Gözbebekleri*').[2]

By the time Nâzım left Turkey in September 1921, the war against the Greeks in western Anatolia was turning in favour of the Turks. After the success of the Battle of Sakarya, Mustafa Kemal needed continuing money and arms from Moscow and agreed to an amnesty for some of the Turkish communists who had been arrested.[3] The following year, however, saw decisive victory over the Greeks, and Soviet support became less essential. In October and November, there was a round-up of communists alleged to have been plotting to overthrow the existing order.

Nâzım Hikmet returned to Turkey in December 1924. By that time the country had become a republic, Ankara was of-

---

1     Göksu and Timms 1999, p. 28.
2     Orhan Kemal includes a quotation from this poem on pp. 90-1. 3 Harris 1967, p. 107.
3     Harris 1967, p.107

ficially the capital and Mustafa Kemal had encouraged the formation of an opposition party. An overtly pro-Moscow leftwing party was functioning and became increasingly critical of the Ankara government. Nâzım returned to Istanbul, still the centre of publishing, and started writing for two pro-Moscow party newspapers, the monthly *Aydınlık* and the weekly *Orak Çekiç*. All this activity, however, came to an abrupt end the following year when there was a clamp-down on opposition activity generally.

This was a reaction to a major uprising in the southeast of the country, led by Sheikh Said of Palu, a prominent leader of the Nakshibendi religious order. Martial law was introduced, and the government was given the power to close down any organisation or publication which it believed to be subversive, and to set up special courts, called Independence Tribunals, to try those responsible. The Turkish Communist Party condemned the uprising, which was ostensibly aimed at the restoration of *Şeriat (Shari`a)*, but also drew on Kurdish nationalist sentiment. Nevertheless, on March 30, 1925, the staff of *Aydınlık* were arrested. Nâzım escaped to İzmir, from where he managed to make his way to Moscow. He was sentenced *in absentia* to 15 years – a foretaste of what was to come. In this instance, he benefited from an amnesty in October 1926, but he did not return to Turkey until July 1928. He then entered the country illegally and was promptly arrested in Hopa, the last port on the Turkish Black Sea coast before the frontier. He was accused of a number of serious offences and was eventually released after six months in custody and returned to Istanbul.

In 1933, after some five years working and writing in the Babıâli, the centre of the publishing and newspaper business in the old city of Istanbul, Nâzım Hikmet was arrested once again for alleged defamation as well as political offences. He was transferred to Bursa Prison – his first spell there – before being released under an amnesty in August 1934. By that time, the international situation looked very different from the early twenties. Turkey had joined the League of Nations in 1932 and was followed two years later by the Soviet Union. The Treaty of Friendship between the two countries had been renewed in 1929, and Ankara was anxious to keep relations with Moscow cordial while continuing to stifle any communist activity within the country. The diplomatic issue which preoccupied Turkey was the renegotiation of the regime of the Straits. Under the 1923 Treaty of Lausanne, which fixed the frontiers of Turkey, an international commission had been given responsibility for managing the shipping going through the Dardanelles, the Sea of Marmara and the Bosphorus. Turkey wanted this changed and applied to the League of Nations. The Soviet Union was not enthusiastic but eventually, in 1936, signed the Montreux Convention, which put Turkey in charge of guaranteeing the free passage of commercial shipping.

The leadership in Ankara was becoming increasingly concerned about the policies and ambitions of Hitler and Mussolini. Good relations with the USSR were again critical. Mustafa Kemal Atatürk and İsmet İnönü (who succeeded him as President in 1938) were determined to avoid repeating the fatal error of the 1914 Ottoman Government, which had entered the First World War on the wrong side.

By 1938, İnönü was seeking a defensive alliance with the United Kingdom and France, but it was seen as essential to continue close cooperation with the USSR. Negotiations began, but before agreement was finalised, the Molotov–Ribbentrop Pact between Nazi Germany and the Soviet Union was signed on August 23, 1939.

This imposed a major change in Turkey's tactics. In October 1939, Turkey went ahead and signed the Treaty of Ankara with France and the United Kingdom. Turkey would be helped by the other two signatories if attacked, and would support Britain

17

and France if they were attacked – but a protocol was added, giving Turkey a get-out clause. It would not be obliged to fight if to do so would involve conflict with the USSR. İnönü seemed to have concluded, before the start of hostilities, that the Allies would eventually win, but he then devoted all his energies to ensuring that Turkey remained neutral until 1945, when Turkey finally declared war on Germany in order to qualify for United Nations founder member status. But the nature of that neutrality shifted as the war progressed.

Orhan Kemal's description of the way the prisoners in Bursa Prison reacted to news of how the war was progressing reflected thinking outside. There was a strong body of pro-German opinion in Turkey, usually associated with the nationalist right, which, like the Camel and his acolytes described in the memoirs, wanted to see Germany win the war. As in the jail, as long as the Germans were advancing, their star was in the ascendant. Government policy was primarily to avoid being dragged into the war but at the same time to ensure that channels were kept open to both sides.

France had fallen in 1940, and in 1941 the Germans had conquered Yugoslavia and Greece and occupied Bulgaria and Romania. On June 18, 1941 a Turkish–German friendship and non-aggression treaty was signed. Hitler launched Operation Barbarossa, the invasion of the Soviet Union, a few days later. This was the period when, in *Three and a Half Years with Nâzım Hikmet*, the Camel and the Azerbaijani gent were dispensing tea, chocolates and boiled sweets in prison to celebrate.

Although Turkey did finally declare war on Germany in 1945, on 19 March the Soviet Union renounced the 1925 Treaty of Friendship with Turkey, and in June Foreign Minister Molotov said the USSR would now demand the installation of Soviet bases on the straits and the return of the two eastern provinces of Kars and Ardahan, which had been in Russian hands from 1878 until

1921. This demand suggested Stalin might have further ambitions in Turkey, and the search for a security vehicle to protect the country against a potentially expansionist Soviet Union came to dominate Ankara's foreign and defence policy in the postwar period. Turkey sent troops to Korea and in 1952 joined NATO. By that time, İsmet İnönü was no longer president: in 1946 he had introduced multi-party democracy as the country started to align itself with the Western Allies, and in 1950 his Republican People's Party was voted out and he resigned to become opposition leader. Nâzım Hikmet was released – but communism was still seen as an acute danger, given the plight of central and eastern Europe and the proximity of an assertive USSR. Nâzım departed for Moscow, leaving friends and family on the other side of the Iron Curtain, many of them unable to visit him.

## From Poet to Novelist

Çukurova is a fertile land, interesting with the major reverberations it has gone through and rich with the contrasts that nurture a novelist. It is one of the places where the first shoots of Turkish industrialisation appeared. It was in Çukurova that the first machine entered the soil in our country... Orhan Kemal's family is also one of the migrant families that made its way to Çukurova.[1]

*Yaşar Kemal*

Çukurova is the fertile Cilician plain around the city of Adana in southeastern Turkey, which was to burgeon in the twentieth century as the centre of the country's cotton production. Orhan Kemal's father, Abdülkadir Kemali Bey, had been born and brought up in Çukurova, and it was in Ceyhan, a small town to the east of Adana, that his son (known to his friends and family throughout his life as Raşit) was born on September 15, 1914.

---

1    Ünlü and Özcan 1991, p. 313.

Orhan's grandfather sent a telegram to Abdülkadir Kemali who was serving as a reserve officer in the Dardanelles,[1] which he signed with the newborn boy's name:

I have come to this world to endure the woes of this world.

*Mehmet Raşit*

As a young man Orhan Kemal's father went to Istanbul and studied law, but politics soon got him into difficulties. He started publishing magazines and writing articles and joined the Committee of Union and Progress (*İttihat ve Terakki Cemiyeti*). In 1912, this led to his being arrested and serving three months of a six-month jail sentence. He nevertheless qualified as a lawyer and became deputy prosecutor in Siirt (in the far southeast of present-day Turkey) and then prosecutor in Basra.

After military service in the First World War, he again became a prosecutor, but in 1919 he stood for Parliament and was duly elected to the last Ottoman Chamber of Deputies which met in Istanbul in January 1920. He moved to Ankara after the Occupation, along with his fellow deputies, and became Under Secretary of the Ministry of Justice and later Minister of Justice, but on November 4, he resigned 'on health grounds', having become aware that he did not have the confidence of Mustafa Kemal. He appears not to have been a member of either the 'First Group' of members of the Assembly (the enthusiastic supporters of Mustafa Kemal) or of the 'Second Group' which broadly fulfilled the role of opposition.[2]

He did not stand for re-election at the general election in 1923, but returned to Adana to work as a lawyer. He also started publishing and writing in newspapers and found himself back in court by December to defend one of his articles. He was acquitted.

---

1    This was shortly before the First World War. The Ottoman Empire entered the war on 30 October 1914.
2    Demirel 2006, p. 56.

In November 1924, a group of Assembly members formed a new opposition party, the Progressive Republican Party (*Terakkiperver Cumhuriyet Fırkası*). Encouraged by this, Abdülkadir Kemali set about founding a different organisation, the General Defence Party (*Müdafaa-i Umumiye Fırkası*). He published its draft manifesto in his Adana newspaper, which was promptly closed by the authorities, and in January 1925 he was given a six-month jail sentence. That made him ineligible to found his new party, which never got off the ground. The Progressive Republican Party was also closed in June 1925 as part of the political clamp-down following the Sheikh Said revolt.

Abdülkadir Kemali Bey then found himself on trial in one of the Independence Tribunals for allegedly having instigated the revolt. Again he was acquitted and returned to Adana to continue working as a lawyer and running his farm until 1930, when politics again intruded. A close associate of Mustafa Kemal set up an opposition party with encouragement from the President, who wanted to see some sort of loyal opposition. It was called the Free Republican Party (*Serbest Cumhuriyet Fırkası*). Abdülkadir Kemali decided to re-enter the political arena – but again on his own terms. On September 29, 1930 he founded the Popular Republican Party (*Ahali Cumhuriyet Fırkası*).

The authorities, however, were finding that the 'loyal' opposition Free Republican Party was becoming alarmingly popular and was threatening the hegemony of the ruling Republican People's Party (*Cumhuriyet Halk Fırkası*). The Free Republican Party was wound up on 17 November. This left Abdülkadir Kemali's Popular Republican Party as the focus of attention and of discontent with the government. Realising the danger, he disappeared, fleeing to Syria.

Six months later, in the summer of 1931, he was joined by his wife and children, and the family moved to Beirut where he opened a restaurant. Abdülkadir Kemali stayed in exile until

1939, when he heard it was safe to return to Turkey. By that time Orhan Kemal was already in jail. Orhan's wife paid this tribute to his father:

> My father-in-law Abdülkadir Kemali Bey was a very wise, experienced, quiet individual. He was never embarrassed about his son's conviction. Through friends he managed to get Raşit transferred from Kayseri to Adana jail. But he realised that because of this the fanatics in the area had become fired up. They were stoning our house and climbing up on carts to rain stones down on our heads. It wasn't working, so he got Raşit transferred to Bursa.[1]

The last word about Orhan Kemal's father, however, should come from Nâzım Hikmet, who included him in his epic poem *Human Landscapes from my Country*. He is given the name Şevki Bey:

> In the first Grand National Assembly –
> that was years ago –
> Şevki Bey would stand with his massive frame,
>       thrusting out his right arm
>                   and ending every speech
>                           by reading this couplet
>                                 instead of a verse from the Qur'an:
> 'In the name of humanity, in the name of faith and
> conscience,
> in the name of the blood shed
> for the right to freedom...'
>
> He was an opposition figure by himself – outside the Groups.
> He was so brave he amazed even Lame Osman.
> They didn't let him stand in the second election.
> He fought.
> He landed in the Independence Tribunal,
> he came out of jail.

---

1   Demirel 2006, p. 321, quoting *Cumhuriyet* 22–24 June 1970.

He fled to Aleppo to continue the struggle from abroad,
and maybe he wasn't brave enough to amaze Lame Osman
any more,
maybe there was a hint of blackmail in this escape.

His whole family went hungry in Aleppo
and Şevki Bey,
    carrying the corpse of a misunderstood hero in his heart
    and with the consolation of believing that even this
        corpse could terrify them,
and carrying a Protestant Qur'an under his arm,
        went back home from Aleppo.

Şevki Bey
rules his home like the Caliphs of Baghdad in fairy tales:
    with his own special, exclusive compassion,
    his merciless justice,
    his unbelievable stinginess and
              generosity...1

Orhan Kemal's mother, Azime Hanım, was also from the Çukurova region. Unusually for a provincial woman of that period,
she had had a formal education at secondary level, and she had
also worked as a primary school teacher for two years. She was
a good talker and an extrovert, with a warm personality and a
good sense of humour. Significantly, perhaps, she was an excellent storyteller and had a very good memory. It is said there was
a strong physical resemblance between Azime Hanım and her
son.[2]

    Adana and the surrounding region were occupied by the
French in 1918. The family moved to a number of towns around
Anatolia throughout this period and eventually reached Ankara,

---

1    Nâzım Hikmet *Bütün Şiirleri* Istanbul, Yapı Kredi Yayınları 2476, 4. baskı
    2008 pp. 1291–1292.
2    Bezirci and Altınkaynak 1977, p. 6.

where Abdülkadir Kemali was a member of the first Grand National Assembly until 1923. Orhan Kemal describes his childhood impressions of the Ankara years:

> When you say Ankara, I remember houses on top of each other amidst a mass of burnt, rotten wood and mud-brick, soldiers and officers wearing kalpaks,1 and children selling the newspaper *Hakimiyet-i Milliye*.2

In 1923, he and the family returned to Adana after the general election. Abdülkadir Kemali, no longer an Assembly member, continued to pursue his political activities, while Orhan was oblivious to the world, enjoying what the rural environment had to offer a child and playing football. Despite the parental restrictions imposed, particularly by his father, it was a happy childhood, and the family did not want for anything.

That situation ended abruptly when his father disappeared into exile and the family was left without any means of support. For the six months before they joined him, Orhan was left to his own devices. The time the family spent in exile in Beirut features prominently in *Baba Evi* (*My Father's House*), the first of Orhan Kemal's semi-autobiographical novels. Following the relative prosperity enjoyed in Turkey, this was the first time Orhan experienced real poverty. Confronted with the need to earn a living, this concern dogged him all his life. It was also in Beirut that he first fell in love with a Greek girl Eleni – and was devastated when she and her family were abruptly expelled from Lebanon.

Orhan decided to return to Adana by himself in 1932, against his father's wishes. Back in Turkey he stayed with his grand-

---

1   The kalpak is a tall brimless hat worn by the Turkish nationalists during the War of Independence.

2   Uğurlu 2002, p. 56. *Hakimiyet-i Milliye* (*National Sovereignty*) was a newspaper published in Ankara from January 1920 as the voice of the Ankara government and later the new Republic. Its name was changed to *Ulus* (*Nation*) in 1934.

mother, supposedly to continue his education, and his mother and sister followed him some months afterwards. He was now totally his own man. Football became his main preoccupation, and he dropped out of school partly in order to devote himself to the game. He played quite well, and his local team had pinned their hopes on him. Orhan and his friends often played on empty stomachs.

That period was extremely difficult for his mother. She had no income, and friends and relatives she thought would be able to help distanced themselves from the family of the man who had dared to defy and criticise the founding fathers of the Republic and their policies. Some were genuinely hostile to the stand Abdülkadir Kemali had taken; some were concerned they might be tainted by association. In 1935, Orhan's mother and sisters went back into exile to join his father, leaving Orhan behind. By that time, Abdülkadir Kemali had moved from Beirut to Jerusalem – then under the British mandate – and was earning a living there working with a local lawyer.

Orhan's family, and in particular his grandmother, believed he might go back to school and finish his education if he was away from his peers, so he was sent off to stay with relatives in Istanbul. Orhan, however, had no intention of going back to school and tried to find some kind of employment with the help of friends from Adana who had arrived in Istanbul earlier. The resulting disappointment and disillusionment meant he was back in Adana within a very short time. He was to use this experience in his novel *Bereketli Topraklar Üzerinde* (*On Fertile Lands*).

Just as he had lost his heart to Eleni in Beirut, Orhan Kemal fell in love back in Adana, but this relationship ended during his short period in Istanbul, as the girl he loved turned her attention to someone else. A brief liaison with an older woman working in one of the bars in the town also ended when Orhan became too serious and the woman left town. Again this experience fed into one of his novels, *Sokaklardan Bir Kız* (*A Girl from the Streets*). Throughout these ordeals his one consolation was books. He read whatever he could lay his hands on: world classics translated into Turkish and work by Turkish writers. He was also writing poetry.

At this time he had started work as a clerk on a very basic salary at the *Milli Mensucat Fabrikası*, a cotton mill producing woven cloth and yarn. It was here that he met Nuriye, whose family had migrated from the Balkans after the First World War. Her family was also poor, and there were a number of well-to-do young men around who sought her hand.

But it was Orhan (or Raşit, as she always called him) who had captured Nuriye's heart, and his plain speaking and honesty persuaded her father. The couple were married on 5 May 1937. Almost a year later, just after the birth of his first child Yıldız, Orhan was called up for his military service and sent to Niğde to serve there for six months. Some fellow conscripts informed on him, and a search of his person and belongings resulted in what was termed 'concrete evidence' of his crime. The charge sheet prepared by the Sixth Army Corps Staff Officer summarises his criminal activities:[1]

Decision of the Final Investigation

I have seen the documents relating to the preparatory and initial investigation of Raşit Kemali, son of Abdülkadir Kemali, from the 12th Infantry Regiment, who has been accused of inciting soldiers to mutiny through engaging in propaganda in support of foreign regimes. In the search conducted after the receipt of information that Raşit was engaged in communist propaganda, items of poetry written in his own hand and addressed to Nâzım Hikmet, a book by Maxim Gorky entitled *Stages and Prisoners from The Russian Revolution* and newspaper cuttings of

---

1    This document is in the archive of Orhan Kemal's family. The Turkish text can be found in Uğurlu 2002, p. 242.

articles on the lives of other Russian writers and on Marxism were discovered. Witness statements of the Niğde library clerk Yusuf, and Adnan, Enver and Hamza from the 6th Company state that Raşit said he admired Nâzım Hikmet and that his works were valuable and should be stocked in the library. Furthermore, Nurettin and Abidin state that Raşit said we were lagging behind European countries like Italy, Germany and Russia and even the Balkan countries, and the documents found in his house were in a similar vein. That is to say, approving of foreign regimes and infiltrating those people with some education and attempting to explain these ideas with examples in such ways as to damage their national feelings indicate that he is engaged in propaganda on behalf of foreign regimes, and his perpetrating these activities within the circle of military personnel constitutes incitement to mutiny. This situation has been attested by the statements of the witnesses and by his admitting to it by the way he tried to explain. Accordingly, as the actions of the accused Raşit fall into the category of Article 94 of the Penal Code, I have decided that the final investigation and the trial should be conducted on x/x/1938 in the Army Corps Military Court in accordance with Article 125 of the High Military Administrative Court Law.

*6th Army Corps Commander*
*M. Ergüder*

That was the document which led to Orhan Kemal's imprisonment until September 26, 1943. The sentence had a devastating effect on his young family as well as himself. Ironically, however, this harsh sentence was to lead to Orhan Kemal's development into a major literary figure in Turkey, with Nâzım Hikmet as his mentor:

Nâzım Hikmet is my real teacher. But it does not mean that he poured the essence of the arts and culture into my head through a funnel.
No! Going back many years I was always keen to read as widely as possible, outside the school curriculum, works which were far above my level. I had thus formed perhaps a rather primitive but quite substantial view of the world and of people. I did a lot of sports, but when I got back home I was a different person, reading a wide range of books. Why I read I do not know, but that I read constantly is a fact. Nâzım

found me almost as a mature adult. He taught me how to look at the world and to see things within the framework of a certain method… People who live in our times, people who can see around them are inevitably affected by the world they live in. The crucial thing is to know how to look. Only if you know how to look can you see what you should see. It is this which Nâzım has taught me…[1]

Orhan Kemal started writing poetry at an early age, and wrote prolifically but ineptly from the mid-1930s. He says his first poem was published when he was in the military prison in Kayseri in 1938 or 1939. It appeared under the name Reşat Kemal. His formative years as a writer, however, start with Nâzım's transfer to Bursa Prison. Nâzım notes his arrival in Bursa in a telegram to Kemal Tahir, who was still in Çankırı Prison: 'Arrived safely.'

The telegram is dated December 5, 1940. The following day, Friday December 6, Nâzım Hikmet sent his first letter to Kemal Tahir from Bursa Prison:

Kemal,

I am in Bursa. The walls, the windows, the concrete walkways of Bursa Prison have not changed since 1933; they are neither worse, nor have they been renovated. I even met a couple of prisoners who have been here since that time. But they found me to have aged a little, as I found them to have too.

I had described this place to you many times. It is a building in the shape of an aeroplane. My room is in the tail end, on the third floor, on the left. It is a little smaller than my room there in Çankırı. There are two of us staying in it. The name of my roommate is Kemal. Yes, 'Kemal', like you. It is not just his name that is similar, he has aspects to his character that are like you in your youth. He is keen on poetry, and he is excitable. He has been sentenced to five years under Article 94. Perhaps he has nothing in common with you other than his name, but I have a need to create this resemblance. Anyway, I am happy with my

---

1    Uğurlu 2002, p. 29.

28

room-mate. Together we can talk about you. He has read your stories which appeared in *Yedigün*. I tell him about you, and thus I feel as if I am talking to you. This 'as if' dimension reached such a point that last night I thought the door would fling open and you would walk in...[1]

This is the beginning of a long correspondence between Nâzım Hikmet and Kemal Tahir which reveals the poet's views on literature, the art of writing, the war, his despair, his hopes, his love for his wife Piraye and then the transfer of his affections to another young woman, Münevver, whom he later marries, his devotion to his friends and his generosity. The letters also provide a valuable account of how highly Nâzım regarded his new young friend in Bursa, depicting the growing closeness between them. Most of the letters make reference to the young man, even if it is just conveying his greetings to Kemal Tahir. Unfortunately very few of the letters were dated, but they were put in a sequence by Kemal Tahir when he was editing them (though certain inconsistencies in the sequence of events suggest that the way they were ordered is not absolutely correct).

Nâzım's second letter to Kemal Tahir sums up Orhan:

My room-mate is a polite young man keen on poetry and literature. For the time being we get along very well. He sends you his greetings.

In the third letter we understand that Nâzım has decided to take his young room-mate in hand and work towards enhancing his education:

I'll tell you how I spend my days now. The doors open at 8 o'clock. Washing, tea-making, wandering about until 9. At 9 sitting down to read a little, or rather to read some stories in the *Berlitz Method* in order to improve your namesake's French...

---

1    Nâzım Hikmet, *Kemal Tahir'e Mahpushaneden Mektuplar* 1968, p. 13-14. Nâzım's letters quoted here are from this book. Nâzım Hikmet was 38 years old at the time, Kemal Tahir was 30 and Orhan Kemal 26.

Two letters, which are some of the few which are dated, provide more information. In a letter dated 3 March 1941, Nâzım writes:

> I do not know what you will think of the short story Raşit Kemali sent you. But he is now working on a new one. If conditions permit and everything is all right, I shall release him into the world in your wake.[1] He is still young and not very experienced. He has to learn a language first. He is studying French. If all is well, in a couple of years time a new story writer will be born into the world...

In a letter dated 17 June 1941, he writes:

> But I should tell you in all sincerity that in my view the record in portraying the manual labourers best is held by Raşit Kemali, whose writings have not yet fully developed.

As mentioned earlier, Orhan Kemal was called by his given name of Raşit Kemali in his close circle. He had his early poems and a few stories published under the pseudonyms Orhan Raşit and Orhan Reşat, as well as under his own name. In 1941 he was asked to send a short story to the literary journal *Yürüyüş*.[2] Concerned that the young writer might get in trouble, the editor published the story under the name Orhan Kemal. From that day onwards all the author's works were signed Orhan Kemal. Publishing under these different names did cause some confusion. Soon after he started using the name Orhan Kemal, Nâzım received a letter from the writer Sabahattin Ali, who was describing his pleasure at the emergence of a new author on the literary scene:

> We have just started to read the short stories of a talented writer called Orhan Kemal. Do you know him? Have you ever heard of him? I very much liked his '*Bir Ölüye Dair*' ('About a Dead Body').

---

1    Kemal Tahir was the more established writer at that time.
2    Kurdakul 1992, p. 135

The letter caused some hilarity between the two cellmates. Sabahattin Ali eventually discovered that Raşit Kemali, Orhan Raşit and Orhan Kemal were one and the same, and the two writers started to correspond. Sabahattin Ali was urging Orhan Kemal to give up poetry and concentrate on prose.[1] But poetry was Orhan's first love and it took some time for him to move away from it.[2]

In a letter to Kemal Tahir dated 25 September 1941, Nâzım Hikmet intimates that minor irritations occurred within the confined space where he and Orhan Kemal found themselves, but the friendship was as warm as it had been from the beginning:

> Each day increases my enjoyment of Raşit Kemali's company. It is not that he does not do irritating things, he does…
>
> Orhan Raşit's going out to work has been very helpful, both for his writing and for the development of his character. Although he makes my blood boil from time to time – just like you used to do, but for different reasons – I am very happy with his friendship, his work and his talent.
>
> I am very pleased with Kemali. Despite everything, his French is improving. He is working on quite a few pieces of writing, and he is advancing with giant steps. I have confidence in him. The progress he made in one year is equal to what could only be achieved in five.

Then we are presented with an exciting piece of news:

> Here is a piece of news for you: Raşit Kemali has brought me a rabbit as a present. His name is Mercan (Coral). He is spotlessly milky white. He is awfully clever and likes human company. I have adopted him as a son. He is very young yet, but when he grows up a bit we shall find him a loyal wife.

---

1 Uğurlu 2002, p. 25.
2 Orhan Kemal says that his first published short story is '*Bir Ölüye Dair*', but Uğurlu says he has established that '*Bir Yılbaşı Macerası*' was the author's first published story in 1941. Tahir Alangu's argument that '*Balık*' has the distinction of being Orhan Kemal's first published short story is discounted by Uğurlu (Uğurlu 2002, p. 21).

Orhan Kemal describes at the end of his reminiscences how he bought the rabbit as a present for Nâzım and the fuss Nâzım made of it, to the delight – and sometimes the annoyance – of other inmates. It certainly seems to have preoccupied Nâzım for some time, as we see a few references to the rabbit in his letters to Kemal Tahir:

> Our son Mercan the rabbit sends his regards to your cat Mahpus (the Prisoner).

But it is perhaps for the best that Mercan is in the end safely removed from the prison:

> I could not convey the greetings of Mahpus Hanım to Mercan as I had to send him to Istanbul to Piraye's mother.

We know that not long after Orhan Kemal left Bursa Prison, Nâzım shared his cell with a bird, a canary. He was always fond of animals, particularly so perhaps in prison. He wrote about this canary to Kemal Tahir:

> I do not know if I wrote to you before. I have a canary. He was hatched here in a broken cage. He is now three months old. He is a bright yellow young man. His mother named him Memo. He is a bit of a devil, very lovable. And how he sings and chatters. He is now in his cage pecking at the strings of his blue stone,[1] but he also keeps on looking up at me, and cocks his ear to the sound of the typewriter. Any minute now he will start singing. Look, he is now standing on the edge of his bathtub.

Nâzım's affection for the bird was such that on another occasion he sent Kemal Tahir a short poem he wrote for his canary:

---

1    This refers to the blue bead believed to ward off the evil eye. It is customary to attach such objects to the cage of a bird or an animal to protect them.

There is only one degree of difference between us,
my dearest canary.
You are a canary with wings who cannot think,
I am a man with hands who can think.[1]

However, before he started to share his cell with the canary, and back when he was still with his cellmate Orhan, Nâzım was thinking ahead to the gloomy day when his young friend would be released:

Raşit Kemali has less than 10 months left to complete his five year sentence and leave here. I am very happy that I met him here. My conscience is at peace for having done my duty by him.

As the time for this release approached it looked as if both men were trying to get as much out of those last days as possible:

Raşit Kemali is going to be the last person and my last output in the form of a human being on whom I will have worked and to whose development I will have contributed. In my efforts of this kind to this date you are my greatest achievement; you cannot imagine how pleased I shall be to see him turn out to be like you. It is because of that I am very particular about his poetry, just as I was about your short stories, and probably more so. More so because poetry is a field I know better, and also because Raşit has made a massive improvement in a relatively short time. When I took him in hand, Raşit was less educated and less cultured, and therefore less prepared, than you had been. He was one of the *Yeni Mecmua*[2] poets. Then he improved substantially in terms of form. But in this developing form there was no content, especially in poetry. His development in content has been slower than the change he went through in poetry. He has not been able to find his own 'voice',

---

1     There is a reference to the canary in Nâzım Hikmet's letters to Vala Nurettin and his wife Müzehher: '... It is 2 o'clock at night. My Memo is asleep in his cage. I am sleepless in my cage.' Nâzım Hikmet, *Bursa Cezaevinden Va-nu'lara Mektuplar*, p. 168.

2     A literary review.

but he will. I am sure of that. At the moment he suffers from the effects of rapid development. I know under what influence he has been writing all these poems, including the ones you particularly like (he also imitates, but not consciously), so I consider his work as yet immature. He and I talk about all this. He will be reading what I am now writing to you, and he will see our frequent discussions sharpened here. Poetry, this tool we are all using, is such a dangerous implement that those who use it have to go beyond being a 'young poet', they should reach another, higher stage. One can get away with being a mediocre story writer or novelist, but a poet is either a poet or he is not. Perhaps I am wrong, perhaps this is a symptom of exaggerating one's own importance through this occupation, but that is what I think, and that is why I am so particular about Raşit's poetry writing.

There were setbacks as well:

A piece of bad news for you: your namesake is not studying French as is necessary, as if it is a duty or a hurdle he has to overcome. I am putting in a formal complaint to you about your namesake on this matter of French. But I have no other complaints about him. In the prison years we have shared together I have had only friendship and comradeship from him.

However, the pace of work quickened again:

Raşit is working like mad. My confidence in him increases with every passing day. But I am afraid for him too; not because he does not have the capacity or ability, but that his self determination, his will may leave him short. If he can control and use his will and his nerves, then there won't be any problems. His path is wide open. He has exactly two months left before he leaves the prison.

I read the letter Raşit wrote to you. He has written beautifully. You write the best examples of letters I have read so far, and your namesake has now shown his talent with this letter of his. Among you, I am the least skilled. But what can one do?

Raşit is getting out soon. Naturally I am very happy about that, very happy indeed. But the pain of separation has already settled in my heart. I have no complaints whatsoever about him as a man, as a friend or as a colleague. I now understand even better how much I have got used to his company and how much I love him. Now it's just you and me again.

Nâzım found that technology increased his productivity:

I am writing to you on my own typewriter. I bought a 1913 vintage typewriter weighing half a ton, which I got on credit. The Ministry of Education insisted that the translation of Tolstoy's *War and Peace* be submitted in typescript, and that is why I had to get this. But I am happy with it, and if I cannot meet the payment I can sell it for a few liras less and manage to save face.

It is wonderful to be able to write on a typewriter, it is the only production tool I can forgive myself possessing on this earth.

Time moved on, and Nâzım expressed a slight concern for Orhan's future:

Raşit has been adding up the days today. There are exactly 136 days until his release. On a Sunday morning in 136 days time he will fly out like a bird. He sends you his greetings. He could not write today as he is extremely busy. I wonder what effect our time together in prison will have on him as against the habits and customs of his previous years. But I am always optimistic about people.

There were also times when even the enormous forbearance of Nâzım was tested:

I shall tell you something very interesting. Apparently there are two spies in Ankara; one a Hungarian, the other a German. They have been sentenced to 15 years each. But they are serving their sentences in a house they rented in the Bahçelievler district of Ankara. A private house with a garden, escorted by a warder and a gendarme, together with their families and friends. What a wonderful country: spies serve their sentences in houses with gardens and those of us who love their country above all else are shunted from prison to prison.

It was now a matter of days before Orhan Kemal was released:

> Raşit is leaving in four days time. My heart burns with the pain of separation. May he fare well.

And finally it happened:

> Raşit has left. May he fare well...
> When he left, Raşit left a huge vacuum behind, one that you cannot begin to imagine. Amongst my young friends I loved him most, after you.
> I have become very isolated here after Raşit's departure. Days go by quickly writing, painting, reading. But there are times when I do not see anyone for a whole week.

And in due course another line of correspondence opened for Nâzım:

> I received the first letter from Raşit. He sends you many greetings.

After his release from Bursa Prison, Orhan Kemal went back to Adana, but it was difficult for him to find a job. There was a reluctance to employ a man who had been jailed for five years. He worked for a few months as a labourer. In 1944 his son Nâzım was born. When a friend in Malatya suggested that it would be possible to find a job for him in a factory in the town, Orhan Kemal moved his family there, selling what few possessions they had. His misfortunes never seemed to end, however; the factory asked for his demobilisation papers, which he had never received as he had been unable to complete his military service because of his imprisonment. The family was forced to return to Adana. In 1945 he was called up to the army and completed his remaining forty days of military service. While financially they just about managed to survive with Orhan taking up various menial jobs, his career as a writer was starting to take off. A steady flow of his short stories appeared in reputable journals and selected short story volumes, and he still published the odd poem here and there. The first volume of his semi-autobiographical novel, *Baba Evi* (*My Father's House*), was published in 1949, as well as his short story collection *Ekmek Kavgası* (*Fight for a Living*). The second semi-autobiographical novel *Avare Yıllar* (*The Idle Years*) followed these in 1950. That year was also the year that Turkish multi-party democracy, which had formally been introduced in 1946, produced a change of government. The general election saw a landslide victory for the Democrat Party, which had been established in 1946. Orhan Kemal had a number of clerical jobs with what would today be called non-governmental organisations. In 1950, jobs in such places were now being given to the supporters of the new government. Kemal yet again lost his meagre source of income. Abdülkadir Kemali Bey, his father, had died in 1949. There was no reason now for him to stay in Adana any longer, and he was desperate to try his luck as a writer in Istanbul, which was Turkey's intellectual hub.

The family arrived in Istanbul by train in 1951. All he possessed was the 400 lira in his pocket, and as a temporary measure they were staying with a former prison friend of Orhan's and his family. As winter approached they rented a house in the poor Fener district of the old city, along the Golden Horn. They had no fuel. Orhan would sit up sometimes late into the morning, so that he could complete a story which he would then try and sell.[1] He was succeeding in selling the stories, although for sums well below what would have been a fair price. He was now a full-time writer, supporting his family solely with writing.

Oktay Akbal[2] describes Orhan Kemal as he was at the time they met:

---

1    Nuriye Öğütçü, *Cumhuriyet*, 23 June 1970.
2    Writer and columnist who became a friend of Orhan Kemal. 50

He had come to Istanbul to settle, but it was a struggle to live in this big city with no means of support other than his pen. He did not have a private income or a salary. He had a wife and children to take care of. He had to write, then to sell what he wrote, and feed and clothe his family with what he earned. In short he was to live by his pen. This was something almost unheard of at the time. To be able to keep to a certain line in literary output, not to debase his art by going for easy options, but at the same time to manage to get money from the Babıâli press and publishers... It was no mean task, but Orhan Kemal succeeded, living in tiny houses with tiny rooms, in poorer districts, and spending time in small coffee houses. He wrote non-stop. He was at his desk for eight hours a day, writing with his pen and later bashing at the typewriter. In a whole generation of writers he was the only one to endure such difficulties and overcome the hurdles. It was a praise-worthy effort.[1]

Soon after the arrival of the family in Istanbul, Orhan Kemal took his wife and children to see Nâzım. It was the first time the poet met Orhan's wife, as she had been unable to visit her husband in jail. It was also the first time Nâzım saw Orhan and Nuriye's daughter Yıldız, whose progress Nâzım had been following through her father's letters and of whom Nâzım had grown to be very fond, despite never having set eyes on her. The two families and their friends spent a happy day together.

Within weeks Nâzım Hikmet was on his way to Russia, and the two friends were never to see each other again. Neither did they have a chance to correspond. Orhan heard the news of Nâzım's death on June 3, 1963 on the radio. He was devastated, and it took him a long time to recover.[2] The best testament to the bond between the two men is the poem Orhan Kemal wrote on the eve of his release from Bursa Prison. Simply titled 'To Nâzım Hikmet' (see p. 161) it starts with quoting lines from Nâzım Hikmet's poem '*Promete, Pipomuz, Gül, Bülbül, vs*' writ-

---

1    Oktay Akbal, *Cumhuriyet,* June 1970.
2.   Interview with Işık Öğütçü, March 2008.

ten in 1929. This homage to his 'master' shows the influence of Nâzım Hikmet as a poet on Orhan Kemal, as well as the impact Nâzım's personality had on him.

Major works by Orhan Kemal appeared regularly throughout the 1950s – *Cemile, Murtaza, Bereketli Topraklar Üzerinde, Grev* and *72. Koğuş* followed each other in quick succession to considerable acclaim. His novels were serialised in newspapers and published in book form almost simultaneously. This productive mode continued to the end of his life. When he died in 1970 he had published twenty-eight novels, eighteen short story collections, two plays and two volumes of memoirs, as well as a book of essays on the technique of writing film scripts.[1] He had also been writing a large number of film scripts. He always claimed he had to write as much as he could in order to look after his family. Orhan Kemal seems to have been incapable of sitting back and writing at a leisurely pace. To save money on fares, he would always walk through the streets of Istanbul. This meant he could feel the pulse of the city and its people. His characters are the small, insignificant people who struggle for survival, whether they are in the cities or in the small towns and villages of Çukurova. He believed that a writer should have a social conscience, but at the same time not lose sight of the artistic merits of what he was creating. He asked himself two questions when considering a plot for a novel or a short story: 'What is it that I want to say to the reader?' and 'How can I say what I want to say?'[2]

He is the first writer to introduce the emergence of industrialisation into Turkish literature through his portrayal of the cotton mills and the exploitation of workers. Before Orhan Kemal, the lead characters in novels were the villagers and the land-

---

1    Gültekin 2007, pp. 27–28. Four of these works are available in English translation. *My Father's House, The Idle Years, Gemilé* and *The Prisoners* (original title *72. Koğuş, Ward 72* in its more literal translation).

2    Ünlü and Özcan 1991, p. 318.

39

owners with their henchmen, or people from the urban middle classes. Orhan Kemal focuses on the relationship between the workers and foremen and the mill or factory owners. He does not gloss over the failings and weaknesses of the characters. Despite the prevalence of starvation, death and misery in his novels, there is hope. Survival is the aim, and somehow that is achieved, and the characters find solace in the hope that tomorrow will be another day.

He portrays women with affection and understanding too. His women mostly work outside the home. They may be poor, uneducated or of easy virtue, but they are strong and they always stand by their men. Children are also prominent in his writing, often part of the work force and exploited, for which society is held to account. Orhan Kemal believed that no one is born bad, and that somehow every individual will find his way to goodness. It is the external factors which traumatise and brutalise the individual.

In his own life, Orhan Kemal was not someone who made excuses for himself, nor did he change his stand for personal gain.[1] Perhaps for that reason he was still being hounded at a relatively advanced age. On March 9, 1966 he was arrested again for communist propaganda. This time it was alleged that he and two others 'believed in revolutionary socialism, that is communism', and had formed an illegal cell using the restaurant of Mustafa Kutlu, one of the accused, to engage in communist propaganda. One incriminating piece of evidence was the book *Nâzım Hikmet'le Üç Buçuk Yıl (Three and a Half Years with Nâzım Hikmet)*. The book was on sale in bookshops, and he had given a signed copy to Mustafa Kutlu. Orhan Kemal refuted the allegations, saying that it was a memoir describing his time in prison with Nâzım and not a eulogy for communism. He

---

1    Ünlü and Özcan 1991, p. 319 (quoting İlhan Tarus).

had been invited to speak at various meetings organised by the Turkish Workers' Party and he had accepted these, and this was also held against him. There was widespread condemnation of the case in literary circles. In the end he was released on April 13, 1966, and at a court hearing he and his co-defendants were cleared of all charges.

The strenuous life he led was beginning to take its toll. He suffered a heart attack in 1967, but could not afford to take the time off work he needed to recuperate fully.

The Soviet Writers' Union invited him to attend the hundredth anniversary of Maxim Gorky's birth, but Orhan could not get a passport. In 1968 he was declared the most successful playwright of the year for his *72. Koğuş*, which played for 372 nights continuously.[1] In 1969 he managed to get a passport for the first time in his life, and went to Russia in response to an invitation. He stayed for ten days in hospital, but left before his course of treatment was completed.

By the early months of 1970 he was feeling much better. He accepted an invitation to Bulgaria and left on 5 May, accompanied by his wife. There he went to see the home town of his grandmother, but his health was rapidly failing. He suffered a stroke and died on June 2, 1970. On June 6, his body was brought over by land to Turkey. At the border point a large number of his friends and those who knew him through his writings were waiting for the arrival of the funeral cortège to accompany it on the journey to Istanbul. As the cortège made its way from Edirne, a worker approached the vehicle. On it he left a simple bunch of flowers and a placard written in oil and tar: 'We the workers bow respectfully in your memory.'

---

1    Bezirci 1977, p. 34.

# THREE AND A HALF YEARS
# WITH NÂZIM HİKMET

It was the winter of 1939–40. I was working in the prison registry, dealing with the record of convictions. One morning, the registrar was checking through the newly arrived documents when he said, 'Oh, you're in luck.' I looked at him quizzically. 'Your master's coming.' I was completely flummoxed. I didn't have a 'master' or anyone who might fit that description... 'Are you messing me around?' asked the registrar. 'No' I said, 'I don't have a master – or anyone of the kind.' 'Look at this, then. Nâzım Hikmet. Isn't *he* your master?' I couldn't believe it. The registrar thrust the document he was holding under my nose. I took it and glanced at it quickly. He really was coming. I noticed the words 'suffers from sciatica. So as to benefit from the baths...' The sky was bleak and overcast that day, and snow had settled on the green leaves of the plants in the prison garden. But after what I'd just heard it was as if brilliant sunshine had suddenly broken through the clouds and swept away the awful numbing tedium, the terrible leaden bleakness of day after day spent so far away from home and the hopelessness of the remaining years of my sentence stretching into the future.

45

Yet I'd never even said hello to the man. And there'd never been any likelihood that I'd one day become his friend. Like everyone else, I was a fan – but from afar. Like everyone else, I was angry at him – without knowing why. But probably, like everyone else, I loved him too, again without knowing why, or having only a very hazy idea why. Those extraordinary verses…

> Look!
> Hey!
> Dumb-cluck!
> Chuck your twanging noise-box.
> That three-stringed fiddle
> with three feeble nightingales
>         chattering on its three strings,
>                 it's quite useless!

> Look!
> Hey!
> Dumb-cluck!
> That three-stringed fiddle
> with three feeble nightingales
> chattering on its three strings
>         can never make the mountains bound ahead,
>                 can never drive forward the waves, the masses!

> That three-stringed fiddle
> with the strength it gets from towns, from villages,
> from rivers yearning to burst their banks,
> can never make the mouths of millions
> laugh or cry with one single voice.[1]

*

> Trrrum,
>         Trrrum,
>                 Trrrum!
> Trak tiki tak!

---

1    From '*Orkestra*' ('Orchestra').

I want to be mechanised!
It comes from my brain, my flesh, my bones!
I'm driven mad by the desire to take over
    every dynamo I can lay my hands on![1]

*

From horizon to horizon
surging ranks of foaming purple waves breaking,
the Caspian speaks the language of the winds, my child,
speaking and swirling!
Who says 'To hell with it'?
[Who says] the Caspian is like a dead lake?
An endless expanse,
just salt water, the Caspian has no master!
Friend and foe
roam the Caspian!

The wave is a mountain,
the boat is a deer!
The wave is a well,
the boat is a bucket!
Up goes the boat,
down comes the boat,
jumping off the back of a tumbling mare
the boat leaps up on to a rearing stallion![2]

*

Hey you!
You, the man with eyebrows like black horns
and the head of sacred Apis;

Hey you!
Knave of Spades! You speak with the noble lexicon of verse,
    I know nothing of nobility.
I decline to raise my hat to the language you speak,
    I am an enemy of nobility
        even when it comes to vocabulary.

---

1    From '*Makinalaşmak İstiyorum*' ('Mechanization').
2    From '*Bahri Hazer*' ('The Caspian Sea').

Hey you!
Knave of Spades!
I know
      the reason for this outburst, these complaints.

I know you're waiting for nightfall
      to strangle me while I sleep.
I who have carried wire shackles on my wrists
as if they were gold bracelets,
I who have looked up at rope soaped and tied into a noose
and have scratched my thick hairy neck,
would I ever be
      intimidated by your threats?[1]

         *

How wonderful it is to live
      TARANTA-BABU
           how wonderful to be alive...

To live, understanding life as a literary masterpiece,
to live, hearing life like a love song,
to live, wondering like a child.
      TO LIVE...

To live:
individually
      and together
         like weaving a silken cloth...[2]

I slunk out of the registry and set off back to my ward to pass on the news to two fellow prisoners who were friends, and who, like me, wrote poetry and thought of themselves as poets.

---

1    From '*Cevap I*' ('Answer I').
2    From '*Taranta-Babu'ya Beşinci Mektup*' (the fifth 'Letter to Taranta-Babu').

48

One of them was Necati. He was my age, but he'd already served five years of a seven-and-a-half year sentence, and had somehow managed to get through those five years without financial assistance from anyone. He'd met Nâzım Hikmet in prison in Istanbul, where they'd become good friends.

Necati was performing cleaning duties in the prison admin unit. I ran into him downstairs by the wire mesh in the visiting area.

'Have you heard?' I said. 'Nâzım Hikmet's coming.'

He couldn't believe it either. I swore I was telling the truth.

'That's fantastic!' he shouted, clapping his hands like a small child.

And then he started talking about Nâzım. About the wooden clogs he wore in the Istanbul prison. About his long, green cardigan. 'Look, we'd better warn İzzet and everyone,' he said, 'so they don't go and start reading him their poetry. He hates being disturbed. They shouldn't pester him with questions. Maybe you shouldn't tell İzzet that he's coming. Otherwise Nâzım will cringe, pick up his bedding and move off to another ward.'

From what Necati was saying, it sounded as if he behaved like one of those 'celebrities'. But whatever... even to meet him – even if we didn't become friends – at least I'd see his face and hear his voice.

I said to myself: I won't go to his ward. I won't ask him anything. And I won't read him any of my poems.

İzzet was reading *Kyra Kyralina*,[1] a book I'd given him. The other prisoners in my ward were all busy doing something. One of them was putting charcoal on the brazier. Another had put his tiny saucepan on the hot coals and was waiting for it to boil. Someone else was sifting through the grains of rice to make sure

---

1    The Romanian author Panaït Istrati's story *Kyra Kyralina* (or *Chira Chiralina;* also translated under the title *Kyra My Sister*) was published in 1923. It became the first of his literary cycle *La Jeunesse d'Adrien Zograffi*.

they were clean before cooking them. Those who weren't doing any work were leaning against the pile of mattresses.[1] One man was reading a newspaper.

Hardly able to contain the hurricane of joy inside me, I sat down next to İzzet. He turned from his book and looked up at me: one of those run-of-the-mill looks he gave me every day, a totally despondent expression, a look that said there's nothing new left to talk about in prison – where every stone, every flower, every inch of the earth has been learnt by heart.

Behind İzzet I could see the mountains through the window. Neither the lake, which was so grey its surface seemed to be covered with lead, nor the snow-capped mountains depressed me that day as they normally would. On the contrary – inside I could feel shafts of golden light and bolts of joy.

'You're very cheerful today,' said İzzet.

'I don't know – am I?' I said.

'You're like you were when you first arrived. What's happened to your usual sullenness?'

İzzet was right. Things had really started to get me down. It wasn't a coincidence. Something had happened three months earlier. I'd become friendly with someone who claimed to be a 'teacher'. He'd told me he'd been forced to break off half way through his studies at the physics department of some university or other in Germany. Never mind university – even İzzet and I knew more about physics than he did. Soon afterwards, the story became public knowledge in the ward and everybody started to make fun of the 'fake teacher'. So duplicitous was his nature that he wouldn't even react – he just smiled ingratiatingly and put up with every insult and slur that was thrown his way.

---

1    The mattresses would be rolled or piled up during the day to save space. This was a common practice in Turkish private houses – even affluent ones – at the time, not just in jail.

As for me, I felt sorry for him. His sentence, though, was short. Every so often he'd be let out under the supervision of a warder. He'd wander around for a bit and brag about meeting and getting allowances from various uncles who were 'members of parliament' or 'officers on the general staff' – uncles we later found to be entirely imaginary. He was so poor and in such a pitiful state that on the days they let him out I'd take off my vest and shoes and lend them to him. He'd go off wearing *my* vest, *my* underpants, *my* coat and *my* shoes, and then apparently denounce me to the authorities. He'd tell them a complete pack of lies. I'd then be questioned and have to make a statement and go through a whole process of totally unwarranted, unnecessary aggravation. And each time he'd join in with my friends in offering his sympathies. He'd curse and swear at whoever it was who'd denounced me. And when he finally completed his sentence and was leaving the jail he burst into tears, fell on my shoulders and embraced me, saying, 'Where will I ever find another friend like you?'

Not long after that – three days later, in fact – I learnt that he was the one who'd been informing on me, concocting a totally inconsistent string of lies. This was the man who'd quite unnecessarily wasted the time of the authorities, who'd worn my vest, my clothes and my shoes, and who, as he was being released from jail, had cried, 'Where will I ever find another friend like you?'

I'd resolved never to get involved with anyone again after that incident. And because one person had degraded himself to such an extent, I'd become hostile to just about everyone. I was probably being unfair in this, but what could I do? I wasn't in a position to think differently, and I didn't really know what it meant to get to know people properly.

And there were other reasons for my depression...

Every day there was at least one stabbing in the prison. People like Nezir the Fisherman, Scumbag Şevket, One-armed Hasan from Antep, İsmail from Feriköy and Mad Mehmet from Konya

51

and their henchmen – not a day would pass without their lying in wait and ambushing someone because of some row over gambling or drugs. The victims had money – and those who didn't have cash were ready to knife anyone to get it.

In spite of Necati's warning, I said to İzzet. 'I've got something to tell you: I've something to tell you, but you didn't hear it from me.'

He looked at me expectantly.

'Nâzım's coming,' I said.

I'd thought he'd be as pleased as I was and would leap up and embrace me. Instead he answered nonchalantly, 'Which Nâzım?'

'Nâzım Hikmet, of course.'

'When?' he coolly replied.

'When? I don't know. The registrar showed me a document about it. And you'd better have heard it from him!'

He shrugged. 'You can be happy about it – why should I care?'

I froze on the spot, amazed that anyone could fail to get excited about Nâzım Hikmet's imminent arrival.

I left İzzet with his *Kyra Kyralina* and went up to the top floor, rushing into the ward where Emin Bey from Sarıyer[1] lived. Emin Bey was a pickpocket who'd told me on various occasions that he'd met Nâzım Hikmet in prison in Istanbul. They'd got to know each other playing chess or draughts, I forget which. Emin Bey was tall and dark and had almond-shaped eyes. He'd pulled his navy blue beret down over his right eyebrow and was standing at the door of the ward, straining some white beans which he'd just been boiling.

'I've got news for you...' I began.

'Eh? Well, out with it, then.' 'You didn't hear it from me...'

'OK.'

'Nâzım Hikmet's coming.'

---

1    Sarıyer is a village on the upper Bosphorus. In those days it was a popular summer resort for the Istanbul population and is now in effect a suburb.

'Get away…'

'I swear it…'

He got up and pushed his beret back.

'You're not winding me up?'

'Honestly. I've just been reading a document from the prosecutor's office. He's suffering from sciatica.'

For a second Emin Bey shook with excitement.

'So… the great Nâzım!'

And he began to tell me his stories from the Istanbul jail. I'd heard them all many times before – in fact I knew them almost by heart. I was desperate for him to finish, so I could go and tell some of the others the news.

It didn't take long – somewhere between an hour and a half and two hours – for the story to get round the whole prison. Nâzım Hikmet was coming – it was in the document from the prosecutor's office.

'Lad – You could never keep a secret, could you?,' Necati commented.

And we started to talk.

'We'll read him our poetry.'

'Nah! What? *Our* poetry?'

'Your poems are pretty good.'

'Yours aren't too bad either.'

'I never went to school.'

'I never finished middle school.'[1]

'Still, you've read a lot. You can even read the old Arabic letters… What about me?'

'You mean he'll pick up his bedding and…'

'He won't stand for it…'

'Did you ever hear him read poetry?'

---

[1]   Middle school followed primary school and took pupils aged between 12 and 15 at that time, although the ages at which individual pupils attended could vary considerably.

'Yes, I did. When he's reading, people are overcome by a swell of emotion. You know, if he takes a crying baby on his lap, it stops crying?'

'I heard this: so the story goes, he'd go into a café, into an ordinary workers' café, with a lot of money in his pocket, of course. He'd approach the poorest man in the place. He'd say "Here's my money. Now you get yours out." The other guy would be taken by surprise and would pull out a few miserable coins. Nâzım would ask, "Why have you got so little?" and the guy would look down at the floor and say nothing. Nâzım would say, "Bring it over here. Let's pool what we've got and split it 50–50." And he'd do just that – pool the money and split it equally.'

Weeks had gone by. It was again a leaden morning. Again there was snow on the leaves... Necati came in, out of breath.

'They've just brought Nâzım Hikmet – a few minutes ago!' As usual I was in the prison registry poring over the record of convictions. I remember the pen dropped out of my hand.

'They took him to the governor's office,' he said. 'I told him about you. Come on – he'll be coming out in a moment!'

He grabbed me by the hand and dragged me along. I was so excited, it was as if the ceiling was spinning round. In my mind I could hear lines from 'The Son of the Kadi of Simavna', 'Benerci' and 'La Gioconda'.

Necati pointed out Nâzım's belongings. They were on the concrete floor in front of the prison admin unit: a mattress wrapped in a check cloth, two scuffed and worn-out leather suitcases, a basket... So he was an ordinary man, just like us? He could think of things other than poetry, worldly things? And he could have a mattress, a suitcase, a basket?

But he must be a 'super-human' being, a genius! Not that I'd ever seen a genius, or had any idea what geniuses were like...

In any case, whatever he might be, the man who was about to emerge from the governor's office would have 'a huge black-sheepskin cap on his head'. No, 'It's not a cap: he's pulled over his head an unshorn sheep cut open at the belly!' Perhaps 'he's sitting cross-legged at the helm.'

And certainly 'He doesn't glance at the waters enveloping the boat; / 'He doesn't glance at the waters cleaving and parting in front of him!'[1]

There's no doubt about it: this man who was about to emerge was clearly 'a statue of Buddha from Turkmenistan'. A marble statue of Buddha, majestically sitting cross-legged at the helm, not deigning to glance down at the waters parting in front of him!

Then suddenly I remembered what Necati had been endlessly repeating: 'He can't bear being disturbed. He'll roll up his mattress and...'

A sharp creaking noise came from the governor's door. And then the door opened. I held my breath. I screwed up my face... I myself was standing as still as a statue, expecting to see an imposing marble statue...

For a split second we faced each other, and then our eyes met... His were smiling deepest blue. This smile reminded me of a child's – pure, fresh, healthy and friendly.

He waited for a moment, unsure of what to do. Perhaps he was looking for a familiar face. Then he must have noticed Necati and was about to walk towards him. But before he could do so, Necati ran up to him and introduced me.

We shook hands. He clicked his heels together like a soldier coming to attention. Trying to look serious, as if he was preparing himself for a formal ceremony, he said, 'I'm Nâzım Hikmet.'

All this happened so quickly... His keen eyes swept around the hall. There were quite a number of people there. Men who'd

---

1    The quotations are from Nâzım Hikmet's poem 'The Caspian Sea'.

known Nâzım from other prisons, and others who knew of him by reputation only... When he caught sight of anyone he knew in the crowd, he'd run up to them. They'd embrace and kiss each other like a father and a son who'd yearned for each other, or brothers who'd been separated for years.

'My dear brother... You – so you're here too?'

'And you're here as well, Vasfi? What happened to your appeal? Did the Appeal Court turn it down? Did they uphold it? Was that after we got transferred to Çankırı Prison?... I'm really sorry. But there was really strong provocation in your case. Nevermind. How are you doing for money? Don't they send you anything from home to help? So the governor's put you to work in the quarantine quarters. That's good...'

He moved on to someone else who was in rags. This man, this 24-year-old man standing with large bare feet on the freezing cold concrete floor was the destitute 'Mad Remzi'. He was one of the inhabitants of Ward 72. That was the ward on the upper floor of the second section which was reserved for the destitutes, prisoners who had absolutely nothing and were on the very bottom rung of the prison hierarchy. All the window and door frames there – in fact all the woodwork – had been torn off, broken up and burnt on the floor in the middle of the ward. That was all the heating there was, and men would throw dice for cigarette stubs in the flickering light of the flames. The windows were all broken, and the driving rain, snow and the bitter cold would blow through the ward all night. The poor wretches huddled together shivering, trying to get warm. 'Mad Remzi' had gone mad in this ward...

' ...then what next, Remzi? So you got thirty years then? What on earth for? You killed someone? How could anyone kill a man in prison, Remzi? What? Because you had to? So you killed him because you were forced to? How could you do that, Remzi? Was it worth it, son? How can a man kill another man

58

for seven liras? Yes, you did something very stupid. But your sentence has gone up to thirty years! That's really bad... Of course, you're human... Why do you curse yourself?'

Remzi hurriedly whispered something into Nâzım's ear. Necati nudged me with his elbow. Predictably, Remzi was asking for 'cigarette money'.

'Later,' said Nâzım. 'I haven't got any change on me now.'

Then he moved on to one of the 'princes' of the jail who was sitting huddled in his fur-lined overcoat. Nâzım asked how he was and enquired whether the knitting machines they used for making socks were still working. And what had happened to the argument with the Black Sea guy in the Istanbul prison about the number of skeins they should use? But the 'prince' had forgotten all about that a long time ago.

Then Emin Bey from Sarıyer turned up.

'Emin Bey! Great to see you, my old friend, my master... my soulmate!' and they embraced. 'So, Emin Bey, it's really you, eh? You here? What did they exile you for? You wouldn't hurt a fly – you wouldn't do knives or heroin. Eh? What happened at your trial? Seven and a half years? Did the Appeal Court turn it down? No, that's unbelievable... But there were mitigating 72 circumstances... Oh well, may the time pass quickly... And what's-his-name's also here, I'm told... Ertuğrul. Here, eh? What a rogue! I've improved my draughts so much, Emin Bey, that I'll certainly beat him now... Dimitri's also here, I gather. I mean the Dimitri of Eau de Cologne fame. I see... So all our friends are here... That's good – good.'

The warder standing next to me – he'd been brought up in a village – said to a colleague of his, 'What a likeable man!'

Meanwhile Emin Bey from Sarıyer asked: 'Master, do you still paint?'

'I've improved quite a lot Emin Bey... Look...'

He went across to where his belongings were in the corner of the hall. The warders had already started going through them. Once they'd looked through his suitcase Nâzım didn't show any more interest in their search. He pulled his suitcase over to where we were and opened it. Papers, notebooks, pencils, paints – oils and watercolours – brushes and then pictures and portraits... various portraits of village people, pictures that had been cut out of X-ray films with a razor blade. He talked about each of these at great length. We all listened, including the warders, even the chief warder. And after a while the registrar turned up, and then the governor.

In their presence, Nâzım Hikmet adopted that peculiar – and rather unconvincing – formal manner he reserved for ceremonial occasions. He turned to them and began his explanation again, frequently repeating 'My master! My master!' Eventually, the governor and the registrar went off to their offices, leaving Nâzım still talking about his paintings.

'And this, this is Kemal Tahir[1]... There's no doubt about it, he's going to be one of Turkey's Finest novelists...' Then he picked up another portrait.

'...they call him Mehmet the Modern... He was the photographer of Çankırı Prison...'

Then another portrait. A village youth with protruding ears, large eyes and a shaven head: 'He's called Mehmet the Headhunter... He's the hero of a major short story by Kemal Tahir.' He turned serious for a moment: 'Our Turkish people are really very clever!'

\*

---

1    Kemal Tahir (1910–1973), former cellmate and close friend of Nâzım Hikmet; a writer who did indeed become one of Turkey's leading novelists (for more details see p. 12).

At that time I wasn't on speaking terms with İzzet – we'd fallen out over something trivial and I'd asked the chief warder to move me to a different ward. He'd given me one of the isolation cells above the same section of the jail, where people who'd broken prison regulations (gambling, stabbing someone or stealing) were kept in solitary confinement until a date determined by the prosecutor's office.

I think it was about a week before Nâzım arrived that I'd moved to cell number 52. They'd prepared another of these cells for Nâzım in the row opposite, two cells down from mine...

Necati, Emin Bey and I picked up Nâzım's mattress, suitcases and basket and flung them over our shoulders. He followed along behind, begging us to leave a few things for him to carry. We went downstairs and upstairs, through several iron doors and dark, acrid-smelling passages. And on either side we passed prisoners who were pacing up and down the corridors in ones, twos and threes with gloomy, solemn faces. After we'd delivered his things, we all congregated in my cell.

Nâzım was talking all the time... He was talking about Çankırı, about the jail and its administration, about Kemal Tahir – particularly about Kemal Tahir and the friendship they shared.

At long last everyone went their way, leaving just Necati, Nâzım and me. Then, without any preamble, Necati said, 'Master, Orhan's written some really good poems!'

I was taken aback and looked at Necati suspiciously...

'No!' I said. 'Not poems, really. Just a few scribbles...'

Necati retorted sarcastically: 'That wasn't what you told us, though, was it?'

To tell the truth, I was proud of my own poems. I had faith in them and high hopes for them. I was absolutely full of them, and before Nâzım's arrival I had been 'the greatest poet' in that prison. Yes, I was, despite İzzet, despite Necati...

'Why do you call them scribblings?' he said 'You'll read them and we'll listen…'

It was lunch time. I got up, lit my little charcoal brazier and prepared *sucuk*[1] and eggs for two. We were about to start eating with our tiny forks from the same dish when Nâzım asked for something else to eat his off. After dividing the food equally, he explained why he objected to sharing the same dish. Scurvy had spread through the villages of Central Anatolia because of this bad practice, he said.

'Where do you get the food from?' he asked, after we'd finished eating.

'From the prison grocer,' I said. 'I have a small notebook, I buy on credit and the grocer writes down what I owe him in the book, and at the beginning of the month, when I get money from my father…'

He took out a small purse and asked, 'How much did you spend on this egg and *sucuk*, for instance?'

'Why do you ask?' I said.

He'd become very serious: 'I want to contribute to the expenses!' He'd taken a two-and-a-half lira note, which had been carefully folded in eight, out of his purse.

I asked him to be my guest just for that day.

'This two-and-a-half-lira note is the sum total of my worldly wealth,' he said. 'If you like, as of today I'll share in the expenses in your notebook and at the beginning of the month…' 'That's fine,' I said.

I don't feel comfortable with people I meet for the first time, especially those who are famous. The reason for this is obvious, but I'm still surprised at how I'd become so familiar with Nâzım Hikmet so quickly, without even realising it.

---

1   *Sucuk* is a dry sausage made with ground meat (usually beef), garlic, salt and spices. It is usually sliced and fried in its own fat.

It's so easy to talk to him – you feel so comfortable...

'You know, I don't like being alone at all. If we could get permission from the administration then I could stay with you in this cell...'

He said this so diffidently. It was as if he'd given an order, or had put me in a difficult position, or as if he'd said something to make me unbearably ill at ease...

'If that's what you want, and if they don't object...' He was very pleased.

'I can't stand being alone! You can't even imagine... I can't write a single word. I just go mad...'

He got up and went to seek permission. The governor hadn't returned from lunch yet, so Nâzım went back again later. The governor discussed it with the registrar and the chief warder and then agreed.

'Oh brother...' Nâzım said, when he returned, 'door after door, lock after lock... It's a bother even to go to the admin unit... How many doors are there here, for God's sake, shutting us in?'

I'd also wondered that in the past. I counted them.

'Six,' I said.

He whistled his disbelief.

It had been less than two hours since Nâzım Hikmet had arrived. In that time, I'd begun talking to him in the familiar singular, and I'd learnt about him and his nearest and dearest: his mother, his wife, his son, his sister, his brother-in-law (who was also his first cousin), his nephews and nieces and many friends. How had this all happened? I don't know. I think in order to be able to understand this, you have to experience Nâzım Hikmet's total sincerity. Because Nâzım is a man who's loved even by his enemies.

\*

I'd been dreading this question, but eventually it came: 'Your education?'

I froze with embarrassment. Every so often, someone would ask me and I'd be so embarrassed as I mentioned my 'certificate' I'd want the earth to swallow me up.[1] It was the same this time.

But Nâzım's reaction was different – he didn't grimace like the others.

'Well, it doesn't matter,' he said, 'as long as you're not planning to become a civil servant... Personally, I've never felt any need for... Do you know any foreign languages?'

'A very little French...'

'Would you like to improve it?'

'Of course...'

'Good... So let's talk a bit about current affairs... For instance, this war, this Second World War, what do you make of it? In other words, what's the significance of these German offensives?'

I embarked on a lengthy explanation. 'Well, you're certainly right on some points... But...'

He ventured further.

'What do you take "philosophy" to mean?'

I'd read quite a lot of books written in Turkish on philosophy and had learnt a number of definitions by heart. I trotted these out one after the other.

He listened to me earnestly. 'It's quite clear you're someone who reads a lot!' he said. Then: 'Your poems?'

I was embarrassed again. My head was spinning.

'They're such primitive things...'

'It doesn't matter. Bring them here so we can have a look at them!'

---

1    Those who left school without any qualifications would be given a certificate to confirm that they had attended classes for the requisite number of years.

My skills as a poet were about to be put to a stringent test. I got up, took them out of my case and brought them over. He put some tobacco in his pipe, lit it, took a few puffs of smoke and said, with great seriousness, 'Yes. I'm listening!'

I started reading...

These were poems written in syllabic metre. Poems where I hadn't expressed my surging emotions simply and sincerely. I'd made them look like the sentiments of poets who claimed 'divine inspiration', and I had articulated them in a comical way, as they had done...

Before I'd even reached the end of the first stanza he was pleading, 'That's enough, brother, that's enough... let's go on to another one please...'

It was one of the poems I'd really felt sure of, and something shattered inside me.

Another poem... I read the first line, then the second. In the middle of the third line:

'Awful!'

My blood was boiling, my head was spinning. I felt so small. Yet another poem...

'Ghastly!'

My eyes were burning... Was I angry? My third poem – I managed to get as far as the first two lines...

'All right, brother, but why all this verbiage and – excuse the expression – mumbo jumbo? Why do you write things you don't really, sincerely feel? Look, you're a sensible person. Don't you realise you're maligning yourself when you write about what you feel in a way that you'd never feel, that you're making a mockery of it?'

My blood drained right down to my feet as I stopped reading and my 'poems' – they were just a bunch of papers – fell to the floor in a heap. I thanked God that neither Necati nor İzzet were around.

Nâzım didn't stop talking... In fact, he was giving a lengthy tutorial, peppered with words like 'realism' and 'active realism', which featured repeatedly... To be frank, I didn't understand a word of what he was saying. Inside, a whole world had been blown apart: a world based on a faulty, cracked foundation, a world made up of mistaken ideas – ideas in which I could never believe – and spurious beliefs which needed to be abandoned!

'And would you now listen to mine?'

I pulled myself together. We were facing each other, eye to eye. 'But you're not just going to be polite about them! You'll also criticise me – mercilessly!'

First he read 'Nigâr and Mustafa'. What I'd been expecting from him was something like the lines in 'The Caspian Sea', a 'Weeping Willow', 'The Son of the Kadi of Simavna' or 'Taranta-Babu'. What he read was different in style from all those. It sounded as if it was spoken spontaneously, consisting of ordinary, simple words strung together. I remember thinking to myself something like, big deal... I could write like that too! And I remember feeling the desire to write in that style beginning to grow and to replace my 'self-confidence' which had just been so spectacularly demolished.

As he read, the pages of the tiny notebook with its black cover were being turned, one after the other. Every so often he stopped reading to explain things... He told me this was 'various sections of a poem I mapped out in Çankırı Prison':

They are as numerous as ants in the earth,
as fish in the water,
    as birds in the air;

they are timid
brave
    ignorant
        dominating
            and they are children.

And those who destroy,
        and those who create
                are they.[1]

Yes, this was different. Very different. This had a language, a quality of greatness which reminded you of holy scripture.

He closed his notebook, took a deep breath and then asked:

'How did you like my poems?'

'Fantastic,' I said. 'Superb!'

He looked at me suspiciously.

'No, you're just being polite...'

He shook his pipe irritably and put his notebooks away in his case.

'You've got what it takes,' he said, 'to become a good writer, that's for sure. I was rather too harsh about your poetry a moment ago... You'll have to forgive me; I'm always very serious when it comes to art or writing... So, that's why... Yes, you've got what it takes all right...'

He frowned and then relaxed his expression... Yet again he filled his pipe, lit it, took a few puffs and exhaled:

'Can I suggest something?'

'Of course.'

'I'd like to take you in hand... I mean with your education... We'll have regular lessons... First French, then other subjects... Could you cope with that?'

'Yes.'

'You give me your word?'

'I do.'

He put out his lightly freckled hand and I held it, noticing his thin, delicate wrist.

---

1    From '*Onlar*' ('They'), the beginning of '*Kuvayi Milliye*' ('The National Forces').

'Without getting fed up, tired or bored...?'
'Yes. Without getting fed up, tired or bored.'
'Agreed?'
'Agreed!'
'All right – that's it then...'
Once again he began chewing contentedly on his pipe.

Days went by. Every now and then brilliant sunshine would tear through the greyness of those days and we'd walk around in the snow in the prison garden.

Nâzım would say, 'It's terribly damp in this prison. It's really bad that we can't exercise properly. Perhaps we should do gymnastics regularly each morning!'

He tried doing this for a few days. He did 'physical training' half naked in his vest in the snow in the prison garden, but after a few days he gave it up...

'Our people regard this sort of thing as weird. They're not used to it... We shouldn't make ourselves look peculiar!'

To be honest, I was relieved... I hadn't said anything to Nâzım, but I'd heard that quite a number of people in the prison had been gossiping and laughing about what he'd been doing.

Every day I'd study for seven or eight hours, sometimes longer. I was also writing poetry 'like his', but at that stage, I didn't have the courage to show it to him. How flawless his poems were, how they could explain so much with so few words! Mine, on the other hand, were wooden through and through, like swallowing something full of fish bones… They were that rough.

Months later, the first poem of mine I showed him was 'A Beirut Story'.

'Read it, let's hear it,' he said.

Gingerly I began:

I'm in Beirut,
in the New Istanbul Restaurant,[1]
standing over the dirty dishes.
I'm eighteen.
My hair is neatly combed and glistening,
I'm thinking of Eleni.

He listened right to the end, his pipe once again in his mouth. Then he took the piece of paper I was reading from, glanced at it and gave it back to me.

'Read it again!'

As I was reading it for the second time, he said 'Stop' and told me to leave out this or that, to move a particular line to the beginning of the poem and to put the opening lines at the end.

While it was being whittled away, I could see a new poem, similar to one of his, emerging from my wooden, stilted arrangement.

He was sparing me a lot of his time, getting into every detail about me, ranging from my 'semi-intellectualism' and my nit-picking nature stemming from my 'petty bourgeois' background, right through to some of my characteristic habits and views…

So much so, that since I became friends with Nâzım Hikmet and started sharing the same cell with him, I'd neglected İzzet and Necati almost entirely. Not that I was on speaking terms with İzzet, but what about Necati?

---

1    This was the restaurant Orhan's father opened in Beirut.

Some time later, İzzet and I made our peace and became friends again. One day, while hiding in a corner of the walkway so as not to be seen by Nâzım, I read İzzet two of the poems I'd worked on with Nâzım. İzzet considered himself just as much of a 'poet' as I was...

He looked disgruntled as he listened.

'Did you write this yourself?'

'Of course...' I said.

Curling his lips, he turned his head away – his hair was glistening with brilliantine – and turned crimson. 'I too', he said, 'I too shall be friends with Nâzım...'

I was most annoyed, and reminded him of what Necati had said about Nâzım's 'getting upset and rolling up his bedding...' But he didn't take any notice.

'I shall show him my poetry too. I'll get him to correct mine as well!' he kept on repeating.

We parted acrimoniously.

I looked for Necati straightaway. When I found him, I read him my poems as well. He liked them very much.

'But,' he said, 'they're not at all like yours... Did Nâzım Hikmet correct them?'

'You know...' I said, trying to change the subject, 'İzzet says... but you said he can't bear being pestered...'

Necati didn't reply, but from that day on, both Necati and İzzet started coming round with huge piles of poetry.

Nâzım listened to their poems carefully, but he never said

'Awful!' or 'Ghastly!' or 'Vile!' like he'd said about mine. From time to time he'd say, for example, 'Bravo, İzzet' or 'This line's very good...' and İzzet would look at me with pride, his brilliantined hair glistening...

After he'd been listening to İzzet and Necati reading their poems one day, I asked him, 'Did you really like them?' He looked me up and down. 'Of course...' he said.

I couldn't help but grimace.

Then one day I said, 'Look, master, you're not doing Necati any favours. He didn't even finish primary school. He thinks he really is a poet. But...'

He nonchalantly blew out a puff of pipe smoke.

'So what?' he said.

'But he doesn't take any notice of anyone. He just says if Nâzım Hikmet rates me highly...'

'Let him say so.'

'Let him say so? Can you really consciously harm a person like that?'

'I'm not doing him any harm...'

'If he believes he's so highly rated, he'll never study to improve himself...'

He stared at me and then laughed:

'I'm sure!...'

Then he just left the cell.

I remained there feeling furious at everyone and everything. The whole world seemed to have darkened. I decided to abandon studying and leave that cell for good.

I put away my books and notebooks. I didn't want the things he was going to teach me. 'I'm sure!...' Huh!

I sat at the window of the cell, looking sulkily at the mountains opposite and thinking of his words: 'I'm sure!...' He'd said it out of spite. And those shits believed him... Of course they couldn't write a word – what they wrote was plainly awful. A single one of my poems was worth all their poetry put together. 'I'm sure!...' Huh!

He came back just as he'd left. I didn't even look up.

'Come on,' he said. 'Are you ready?'

He was going to check my French, but I didn't take any notice.

'I'm talking to you!' he said.

'I'm not ready!' I said, turning away and trying to appear nonchalant.

He didn't insist at all.

'Fine,' he said, 'get ready then.'

He left the cell. Later, when my anger had subsided, he asked again, 'Are you ready?'

I muttered a few things, some sort of excuses, explanations…

'We come from the same stock,' he said, 'I know you as well as I know the palm of my hand…'

Then one day he gave all three of us – İzzet, Necati and me a poem consisting of six lines.

'Change the order of the lines,' he said, 'and put this poem into the best possible form.'

Each one of us, working in a separate corner with the utmost concentration, tried to give the poem the 'best possible form' by changing the order of the lines. We fully realised that this was a test, a contest between the three of us.

Each of us had decided on a different 'format'. We, the three rivals, all three in trepidation, all three of us hating each other, our eyes fixed on Nâzım, gave him the sheets of paper we'd been writing on.

Nâzım took them, read them and considered them at length. Finally he said, 'Good! Good for you, this is the best…'

*I* had won the contest.

75

Another day, having somehow got hold of the opening pages of a novel of mine, he rushed out to me in the prison yard, wearing his clogs, terribly excited.

Breathlessly he asked, 'Did *you* write this?'

Hesitantly, I said yes.

'Look here', he said, 'why didn't you tell me about this? You should write prose, yes, prose!'

I was amazed... He talked to me at length and then asked me to try my hand at a short story. In Turkish literature, short story writing was probably the genre I was least familiar with; I didn't know much about it, never having involved myself with its rules and principles.

'So much the better,' Nâzım was saying. 'You'll be able to find your own voice, your own style without being influenced by anyone!'

I had now put poetry on the back burner. The lessons continued apace, and the foundations of my short story writing were being laid.

'Ask me,' he'd said, 'ask me whatever comes to your mind...
Appropriate or not, relevant or not, timely or not...'

'Was this what Freud had meant?'

' ...and Stendhal and Zola and Balzac...'

Then one day, out of the blue I asked him this:

'Master, they say that when you were outside, before you
were in prison, you'd go into a café, seek out the most poverty-
stricken man in the place, take your money out of your pocket
and then say to him: "Now you take out your money too!" The
man would take out a few coins and you'd then pool them and
divide the money equally between you.'

He listened to me with astonishment, growing more and
more angry. I'd expected him to laugh and perhaps come up
with other similar examples.

'Never,' he said. 'I can assure you, on my honour... that I
have never behaved in such a frivolous manner!'

Another day I asked him something else.

Someone had written an article in *Yeni Mecmua*[1] in which he
said that Nâzım was so ignorant that 'he would not understand
Fikret'.[2] The writer had argued that the free verse style was not
original to Nâzım, but that he had taken it from a Russian poet
called Mayakovsky.

I'd read this article a long time before I met Nâzım.

'Mayakovsky's fragmented lines are indeed rather like mine,
but he writes in a kind of prosodic metre, in Russian prosody...
whereas mine are pure harmony...'

---

1    The title of a major literary review of the pre-Republican period, which
     published some of Nâzım Hikmet's earliest poems. It was closed after the
     founding of the Republic, but literary magazines with the same title sub-
     sequently appeared at various periods, including the early Second World
     War years. *Yeni Mecmua* means 'New Magazine'.

2    Tevfik Fikret (1867–1915) was the most distinguished Turkish poet of his
     generation. He was the first to introduce Western forms into Turkish poetry.

And then he went on to explain how, during the War of Independence, Vala Nurettin, Yusuf Ziya, Faruk Nafiz and he had set off for Ankara. The Ankara Government had forced Yusuf Ziya and Faruk Nafiz to turn back, Faruk Nafiz for writing eulogies for the Sultans, and Yusuf Ziya for...

The plight of Anatolia at the time, its abject poverty, affected Nâzım deeply. He wanted to write about it... There was a lot to say, but the possibilities offered by prosody and syllabic metre were very constrained... Then he came to think he needed to break free from these set forms and to try and find other poetic vehicles that would be more free, and broader and stronger. Or rather he felt, with a burning urgency, that the syllabic and prosodic forms which were adequate for expressing minor, simple, insignificant feelings were too restrictive for a broad and all-encompassing content.

Not just a few,
not just five, ten,
thirty million
starving are
ours!

They
are ours!
We
are theirs!...

The starving are lined up – the starving!
Neither man nor woman, neither boy nor girl,
thin emaciated
    twisted gnarled trees
        with twisted gnarled branches!
Neither man nor woman, neither boy nor girl,
thin emaciated
    twisted gnarled trees
        with twisted gnarled branches!

Neither man nor woman, neither boy nor girl
The starving are lined up – the starving!

Some are beating
their knees which are just bone
                        and carrying
their swollen bellies!
Some are just
        skin... skin!
Only
their eyes
                are alive![1]

This poem is the expression of the emotion he probably experienced first in Anatolia, and then when he encountered the hunger and poverty along the Volga River immediately after the Revolution.

And then Moscow...

'For days and indeed weeks on end,' he would say, 'I toiled to broaden the possibilities of poetic expression through new voices, new means of articulation...'

Then, while he still did not know any Russian, he got hold of a Russian newspaper and for the first time saw the 'smashed up lines'! Realising that this might be a poem, he got a friend of his to translate it. The passage was indeed a poem, and one by Mayakovsky... That had been his introduction to the poet...

Every day the same walls, the same faces, the same window and the same mountain, the same hillsides as seen from that same window... Everything stays the same, except nature, which changes with the passing seasons... Sometimes I'd sit in front of the window and gaze outside: right out into the distance, a villager ploughing very slowly under the hot sun, or a young girl on a road which meanders through the fields with her lunchbox in her hand...

---

1    From '*Açların Gözbebekleri*' ('The Eyes of the Starving').

The most enjoyable and entertaining days in the prison were most certainly the major religious festivals, the *bayrams*, and also the visiting days. But particularly the festivals... Just as in the outside world, everyone would try to get something new to wear. On the eve of the festival, even those with the least money would tip the barber's apprentice after they'd had their shave and then leave quietly laden with the weight of the pleasure they could barely contain. On those days even enemies would make their peace, most of them... Those who'd try, for eleven months of the year, to earn a living by gambling and dealing in opium, hashish and all kinds of other 'banned' substances, and who would be prepared to drown each other in a spoonful of water on every single day of those eleven months in order to be able to do so, would be immersed in 'brotherly love' during those three days of festivities.[1] Cigarette packets would be brought out and shared, visits would be paid, tea would be brewed, or someone would be persuaded to brew it... And the destitutes would gorge themselves on food and cigarettes...

It was the first such festival or *bayram* since Nâzım and I had become friends. We went to the prison barber's on the day before the festival, where he had his haircut and shave before me. And as I was sitting in the chair he vacated, he stood looking at himself in the elderly barber's dirty mirror – the barber had been in jail for fifteen years – inspecting his haircut and scrutinising his shave.

The barber's apprentice, a healthy looking village boy of fifteen, offered him the tray. The lad had taken the cigarettes out of a packet of twenty Köylü and put them on a coffee saucer, and there were coloured *bayram* sweets in another saucer. There was also a bottle of Çoban Eau de Cologne.

---

1 . The festival in question is clearly the *Şeker Bayramı* or *Ramazan Bayramı* which follows the fasting month of Ramadan.

For form's sake, Nâzım took a cigarette from the tray. The apprentice insisted he take a sweet as well and sprinkled some Eau de Cologne on his hands.

It was customary to leave a tip... And Nâzım was no doubt aware of this... He rummaged diffidently through the pockets of his red striped pyjamas and then laughed, 'Oh, damn it!'

We looked at each other in the mirror...

'All right, all right...'

Nâzım had wanted to give an appropriate tip and had put his hand in his pocket to do so, but his telling look revealed he was denied this pleasure... Or was that my imagination?

There was a southerly gale blowing... heavy, hot and howling...
Doors were banging, window panes were being smashed somewhere, the trees were soughing in the wind...

It was well beyond midnight. The Japanese clock that Nâzım
had bought in Beyoğlu[1] some time or other showed two o'clock.
I was studying God knows what, and he was sleeping. Then suddenly he jumped up, threw back his cotton quilt and bedding,
his blue eyes full of sleep...

'Can you give me your pencil?'

I gave it to him and waited, wondering what he was going
to do. He wrote something on the wall by the head of his bed,
returned the pencil and, with great solemnity, lay back down on
the bed and pulled the bed clothes over his head.

I got up gingerly and read what he'd written:

On the loneliest of waves
an empty tin can.[2]

---

1    Beyoğlu is the quarter of central Istanbul which in those days was the
     principal fashionable shopping area.
2    The third and fourth lines of '*Lodos*' ('Southerly Gale'), one of a num-

The next day I heard his clogs clattering as he paced quickly up and down the walkway. I realised that once again he was thinking about poetry... I went and stood at the door of the cell. This blond apparition was weaving his way around, muttering and emitting a droning sound, rubbing his forefinger against his thumb as if he was sprinkling uncooked noodles into a soup. He'd bump into other prisoners who were walking up and down in twos or singly, and then he'd pull himself together and make a gesture with his hands to apologise, and then again I'd hear the same droning sound, the same noise of him pacing up and down, now the full length, now a short stretch, and then abrupt turns... Now and then he'd dart into one of the cells and then dart back out again. Then I thought he was looking for me, but I was standing by the door of the cell; he couldn't see me inside, but stumbled upon me as he was rushing out. He stared at me anxiously as if he'd forgotten what he was going to say. He just about managed to say, 'Your pencil, please,' and by the time I'd taken it out he'd already gone off to walk another length of the walkway. Then he made a sharp turn, and as he passed me I held out my pencil. But he'd already forgotten about it and carried on walking. Suddenly he seemed at a loss, then he took the pencil, bowed solemnly to me in acknowledgement and carried on clattering down the walkway in his clogs.

'The most infuriating thing,' he used to say, 'is to be looked at by everyone when I wander around "totally lost." I'm worried they'll say I'm mad. So I can't just let myself go completely.'

---

ber of poems written in Bursa Prison. It is dated 23 January 1941. See Nâzım Hikmet, *Bütün Şiirleri* (Istanbul: Yapı Kredi Yayınları 2476, 4. baskı 2008, p. 707 ff ). An English translation of the poem can be found in Nâzım Hikmet, *Beyond the Walls: Selected Poems*, translated by Ruth Christie, Richard McKane and Talât Sait Halman (London: Anvil Press in association with Yapı Kredi Yayınları, 2002, p. 130 ff ).

One day, at some place where he was a guest – I think it was a relative's – he apparently got the urge to write a poem. He started walking up and down diagonally across the room, reciting aloud and getting more and more excited. A young servant girl saw him and rushed to the lady of the house and said, 'Please madam, I think the young master has lost his marbles!'

Certainly I can confirm that Nâzım was prone to excitement. He would divide his day into chunks, and if he was supposed to write at a particular time he'd gear himself up and get down to work.

Even Nâzım's rhymes have certain functions within the entirety of the poem.

Anything to do with writing or art he took very seriously, and he regarded the writer or artist as bearing a heavy responsibility. The writer or artist is always accountable to the working masses.

He was diametrically opposed to the theory summed up in the expression 'Don't be duped: every word uttered by the poet is a lie!' With Nâzım, that became 'Believe me – every word uttered by the poet is definitely true!'

Nâzım believed that the poet is 'the engineer of the soul'.

He had the utmost respect for hard-working people. In prison, people kill and get killed, you come across people who hurl obscenities at you about your mother, your sister, your wife, and men who swear and blaspheme about God and the Holy Qur'an. Nâzım would go down to the workshops of prisoners who had more useful things to do with their time than taking drugs, gambling and stabbing people. If he got the chance, he'd do some job there – planing a piece of wood, weaving some cloth...

Some people might interpret such actions as serving some hidden agenda, but as I see it this should be regarded as nothing more than an example of the respect he had for his fellow man, and of the value he put on those who created something, who really took an active part in production. I should also add that, contrary to what is widely assumed, Nâzım was not a strident individual who argued and engaged in propaganda at every opportunity. He always showed the greatest respect for other's opinions, and did not engage in arguments unless he was forced to, and many a time even if he *was* forced to...

Nâzım was a believer. He respected people who believe in a cause, whatever it might be. That's why he respected Mehmet Akif[1] – not because he agreed with his views but because he appreciated Akif for being 'a man of character' who believed in his cause.

There are people who are ideologues. They claim to be following a set of rules and ideals, but in practice they find them-

---

1    Mehmet Akif (1873–1936), poet and writer celebrated as the author of
     the poem which became the national anthem of the Turkish Republic.

selves to be diametrically at odds with their principles. Nâzım tried to put theory into practice.

He had an unbounded affection for the human race. So much so that he made that into a 'religion'. He had a special affinity with children... I never witnessed an occasion where he stopped a child crying by picking it up and comforting it, but I can assert categorically that any child could be 'friends' with him.

One day I wrote a poem with that side of his character in mind and showed it to him.

I said, 'I ascribe all this to you, master!'

He took it and read it. His nostrils were quivering as he did so, and it was clear he was trying hard not to laugh:

To be able to roll a hoop at the age of forty,
to be able to blow soap bubbles in the air,
to steal jam from the larder,
to spy on the neighbour's daughter through peepholes!

Red rose jam served on a spotless silver spoon,
that's childhood.
To be able to roll a hoop at the age of forty,
to be able to blow soap bubbles in the air!
To be able to love the world and people,
to be able to love in spite of everything,
to be able to love, to be able to love...
To be able to blow soap bubbles in the air!

'As a poem it's good,' he said, 'but am I really that weird?'

'I was trying to get a flavour of you across...'

'Yes, but just imagine a forty-year-old man chasing a hoop through the streets in short trousers! Or think of a bloke sitting on the stone floor like a lunatic, with a bowl between his legs and a large bar of soap in his hand, all right, blowing bubbles in the air...?'

'No, no, that's not what I was trying to say,' I said. 'Imagine, for example, mankind totally free in his battle against nature.

He's rid himself of all his parasites, and the world has turned into paradise...'

He didn't reply, but his silence was such that that it forced me to reconsider... Yes, in the 'days of paradise' forty-year-olds will certainly have a lot of time on their hands, but they won't be so unhinged as to run along the streets rolling hoops, nor will they be so mad as to blow soap bubbles...

I carried on asking him whatever came into my mind. I had some rather serious, bespectacled, philosophical-looking questions to ask, but there were other questions that were only mock-serious, light-hearted, more the sort of thing you'd associate with a third-rate music hall.

It was from Nâzım that I learnt all the minute details of the Babıâli[1] and Ankara Caddesi,[2] which I remembered walking along a few times with my father, and I felt that if one day I found myself walking up that famous thoroughfare again, I wouldn't feel surprised at all.[3]

I used to buy various newspapers regularly as a child, making a collection of them without really knowing why. The collection changed, as I grew older and my reading broadened, into

1 Babıâli literally means 'high gate', but the conventional translation is 'Sublime Porte', and as such it referred to the headquarters of the Ottoman Government in the centre of the old city of Istanbul. But this particular quarter was also the centre of newspaper and book publishing, and Babıâli is employed here rather as 'Fleet Street' is used in English. (Since the eighties, publishing has mostly moved out to the modern commercial areas on the outskirts of the city, and the Babıâli, again like London's Fleet Street, is no longer a magnet for journalists and writers.)

2 Ankara Caddesi (Ankara Street) is a wide, steeply sloping thoroughfare which leads up from the Sirkeci railway station by the Golden Horn into the middle of the Babıâli quarter. It continues up the hill, changing its name to Babıâli Caddesi. It eventually meets the Divan Yolu, the principal artery of the Ottoman (and Byzantine) city.

3 Orhan Kemal writes in a footnote here: 'Indeed I did end up there. And it never felt strange. But that's another story.'

sports magazines. Later on they in turn were replaced by literary magazines.

I'd give money to the warders or the prisoners who were let out to work under provisions of the Labour Law to buy me literary magazines. A number of these magazines were publishing poems that reflected the new literary trends, bereft of metre, rhyme and harmony. Having learnt reams of rules for writing poetry, I didn't set much stock by things which came across as having been just thrown together, things which didn't look as if they were the results of painstaking work. İzzet and I had always poured scorn on them... We'd mocked them, but we both believed that something must emerge from this...

İzzet and I thought we'd written a lot of 'poems' like these. It was only after I met Nâzım that I understood the difference between the conscious construction of 'new poetry' and our attempts that were merely derivative; between their language and our crude and wooden, rough-hewn voices.

What I mean to say is that, leaving aside its brevity and immaturity in terms of content, in order to get to the stage of being able to enjoy the taste of the new poetry, its language, and in particular its natural quality, you have to divorce yourself from the old, worn-out, putrid, insincere 'theorising'.

Those who cannot shake off the influence of *Edebiyat-ı Osmaniyye* ('Ottoman Literature') and *Talim-i Edebiyat* 'Teaching of Literature'),[1] and those who cannot move away from the literary tradition which more or less follows the same route and seeks to make others follow it, cannot understand this new kind of writing, and we have to make allowances for them.

Nâzım was very open to the process of simplifying the language. Nevertheless, he himself tried not to go to extremes.

---

1    These are manuals setting out the principles of Ottoman literary traditions and the teaching of literature.

'In language, it should be the people that we measure ourselves against. We should be careful not to use words which people don't use every day and don't feel comfortable with,' he would say. One of the new words he liked most was the word *olağanüstü* ('extraordinary'). He used this word a lot. He loved words which were a combination of originally Turkish words and ones which people used colloquially. He was against discarding words – Arabic or Persian – which people had adapted to their own usage and moulded to the shape of their own language. He didn't believe they should be replaced with words taken from French or Chagatay, or some 'concocted' vocabulary. And I've no doubt that he believed the Turkish language would be developed not by top-down commands, but by writers of literature. Nevertheless, he was ready to admit that a lot of the words the authorities had tried to impose had gained wide acceptance, even if a large number had been discarded. But on balance he thought the words formally introduced did have their uses.

He was very interested in the new trends in poetry, and although he was very sympathetic towards young poets, he would say that what they were doing, or rather what they were trying to do, was not something new.

He accepted that poetry could be written by throwing aside metre, rhyme, harmony and even meaning, and he would go even further and accept that poetry could be composed without writing, purely through a set of thought processes. 'But,' he'd say, 'why do we need such radical reduction? Why shouldn't we make use of the opportunities poetry has benefited from through all its centuries of development? This is just supposing that new things can be made through forcing the form. The issue has more to do with content rather than form, with innovation in content. The avant-garde represents the weariness of a class which has lost its hopes and its ideals, which has degenerated or is heading towards degeneration. They represent its wish to shy away from the world – and this is rooted in being defeated by reality – and death, in particular they represent death... They're allowing themselves to be carried along by a strange exoticism, they do not involve themselves in the great causes of humanity, or they lack the courage to do so! The only positive thing about them is their language. They use the language very well – although in a limited way. Their poems are segments that have fallen off a huge piece of work...'

Nâzım was always very aware of the boundary between poetry and prose. In his work entitled *Human Landscapes from my Country* you'll see that he's brought poetry as close to prose as is possible, and that he makes use of all that poetry has gained up until now.

By the spring İzzet had served his time and was released, and it would soon be Necati's turn... I still had years to go. Despite all the differences we'd had, I regretted İzzet's departure. Necati was benefiting from the Labour Law – out all day with the rest of the prisoners working as labourers...

We were no longer playing football.

The prison grounds were ideal for football. And we found out that it had always been the usual game for prisoners to play. But from time to time, the chief warder would try and stop us from playing, pointing out that it was possible, though very unlikely, that the ball could be used for drug trafficking, by being kicked over the wall and then kicked back in again. That's how he'd try and take away our only means of recreation.

On those afternoons when the chief warder could be persuaded to let us play football we'd go down into the garden in two teams. The other prisoners would crowd behind the iron grilles of the prison windows in a festive mood and yell at us just as they would at real games saying, 'Come on!' 'Bravo!' 'Shoot!' 'Stop him!' and all that.

We used to play before Nâzım arrived, and we were rivals on the pitch, much as we were in poetry. İzzet and Necati played really well. Especially İzzet... As for me, I was such an addict that I'd exchanged school for football – maybe it wasn't the only reason, but it was the main one.[1]

To cut a long story short, a tall, blue-eyed forty-year-old poet with curly blond hair joined us one day. He was playing in the most difficult position in the team: centre-half!

Quite often, İzzet and I would be playing against Nâzım's team. I'd play centre-forward and İzzet inside-right, or vice versa. Because he wasn't as good at football as he was at poetry, and didn't have the same lung power, we'd easily break through his defence. This would infuriate him. He'd get so upset... He'd pull the peak of his grey cap round to the back in anger, move to centre-forward, admonish the halves and the backs and rearrange his team on the field, but despite all that, once the game resumed, it wouldn't be long before İzzet and I would pass the ball to each other, bear down on their goal and... score!

He'd be livid... His face would go scarlet, his eyes bright blue, his blond eyebrows disappearing into the bright red expanse of his face... And if we tackled him and got the better of him, he'd become the worst of all foulers and have a go at us, kicking, punching, elbowing. I once got a rather firm boot from him. To be honest, it was quite a splendid kick...

After Necati left we had to give up football. In any case, the outer leather casing of the ball and the rubber bladder inside were both in tatters, and a bitter winter had set in.

My lessons were continuing at a steady pace. But at times I got so exhausted with the weight and seriousness of the les-

---

1    In his semi-autobiographical novel *The Idle Years*, Orhan Kemal describes how his passion for football was one factor that led him to drop out of school.

sons that I'd almost feel like exploding between those stone walls. He'd be the same... I'd look at him, lying on the bed with a book in his hand, then he'd give up reading and before he hurled the book away we'd just stare at each other, thinking the same thoughts born out of the same boredom, without uttering a word... We talked so much... Especially when the sky outside was grey and it was snowing heavily, or when the cold days just went on interminably between those stone walls, when the raw intensity of the cold was increased two-fold... Look to your right, there's a wall! Look to your left, there's a wall! Look in front of you, there's a window, with the snow hurtling down outside! If it's not snowing, you'll see the same bit of mountain, the same sky, the same hillsides... The morning starts with a leaden weight with a leaden weight it turns into midday, and then it becomes evening, still with the same heaviness... Deep down somewhere the ceaseless cacophony of the jail permeates everything and goes on until nightfall, when the sound of the warders' whistles echoes against the cold, naked walls and draws harsh lines on the howling night of the prison, when the doors of the wards are barred and locked from the outside...

At the windows, the darkness of an abyss. Men deprived of women, trying desperately to sleep, tightly closing their eyes, so full of longing. Nights that never end...

The nights are one thing... But the days... I know such days only too well. On such days, not just in jail, but even outside, at times when I get carried away by the idleness of 'streets full of freedom', the negatively charged atmosphere really gets me down.

At moments, we'd catch each other's eye, when we just stayed there without saying anything, Nâzım would sigh deeply and mumble, 'Hell... I've got twenty more years!'

And then all of a sudden he'd shake himself and get up and look for his pipe. Still depressed, he'd fill it with tobacco, then light up and frantically start puffing. Finally he'd look at me again with despair in his eyes.

'Well, it can't be helped...' he'd say. 'Get on with it. I mean, take out your French...'

His problem wasn't just the leaden dead weight of each day, as it was with me. I had my father to look after my wife and child. In fact, my father took care not just of my wife and child, but of me as well. But Nâzım?... The help he got from his mother and his sister was just about sufficient for his own needs... But he also had a wife who didn't get any help from anyone, and there was his friend Kemal Tahir...

In one of her recent letters his clever, emotional, highly sensitive and thrifty wife, Piraye Hanım, had mentioned that she was worried about not being able to buy wood to burn that winter. She was afraid her daughter had tuberculosis and she wouldn't be able to afford her proper treatment.

I knew how thoughtful a person Piraye Hanım was, and I'd heard directly from Nâzım many examples of her selfsacrifice, so

I realised that if she was compelled to write to her imprisoned husband in such desperate terms she must really have been in dire need.

For days on end, Nâzım wandered around subdued, preoccupied and downcast. On one occasion he said, 'In this prison, on the walkway in that section two, I once collected fag ends and spent forty-eight hours with nothing to eat but dry bread, yet even then I never felt as desperate as I do now!'

One day Ertuğrul, who was in the same ward as we, came up with a proposal. He'd been convicted for pickpocketing and sentenced to eight years and two months, even though the sum total of the money he stole was no more than a couple of hundred liras.

'Look here, master,' he said, 'I've got an idea, but I don't know, what do you think?'

The idea was practical: we could buy a couple of looms and set up a weaving workshop. One of the prisoners due to be released in a few days had looms for sale.

It came just at the right time... Nâzım mulled it over and made various calculations... He walked up and down the walkway for a while with his pipe in his mouth... He must have found that the idea made sense, because during the course of the next few days he contacted the governor, the registrar and the public prosecutor who dealt with the prison and made representations to them. He managed to get the necessary permissions and got things set up. In a few days time, with the addition of another loom brought in from outside, three looms were made ready to work. The major hassle was obtaining the yarn, which was subject to rationing and, as far as I can remember, only two packs were allocated per loom, and only to those looms which had been registered with the cooperative by a certain date... Looms set up after that date couldn't avail themselves of this concession.

The yarn was bought, and there in front of Nâzım's pipe, which was now happily emitting clouds of smoke, and his nostrils, which were quivering with the joy of success, the looms started up. Nâzım could hardly contain himself. With all the clacking of the looms it was like being in a factory. Nâzım was running from right to left, from one loom to the other, watching the shuttles shooting around at the speed of bullets, the weavers working with their hands and feet simultaneously, checking the bleaching and stiffening processes, sometimes looking surprised, sometimes explaining things and every so often talking about 'production'.

Although I hadn't been involved in this loom business, either at the planning stage or in putting up the capital, Nâzım had

nevertheless set aside a share for me as well; one share for me, one or two shares for Kemal Tahir, one share for Ertuğrul, two shares for Piraye Yenge, and one share for himself...

The sheets, the towels and various types of cloth that were woven were sent off to the weaving cooperative. We just got paid for the weaving. On the days when our cloth was delivered to the cooperative and the money came in, Nâzım would become a serious accountant; he'd sit at the table, wearing his spectacles, and with his pen in hand and notebook in front of him, he'd begin a series of calculations... He'd work out everyone's share meticulously, down to the last penny, and he'd grab the first opportunity to get Piraye Yenge and Kemal Tahir's shares into the post to them.

Now he was being addressed as 'the Boss'... 'Master, so you've increased the work, eh! How? Well, you see... that's what money does...'

And so on and so forth...

He'd deal with all this in good humour. 'Of course, of course', he'd laugh, 'I've become the big boss, and now my character's been corrupted.'

'There's no hope for you...' I'd say, pulling his leg. 'Too true,' he'd reply. 'Unfortunately that's what's happened. There's no hope for me now. I'm not worth anything any longer.'

Nâzım used to concern himself with all the needs and problems of the people he worked with. The young men from western Anatolia who were weaving cloth at the looms had come to be devoted to him. This, for some reason, had made others who had their own looms suspicious. Nâzım couldn't care less... He carried on regardless: the cloth went on being woven, metre after metre.

Then we heard on the grapevine that a land-owner from some village or other was plotting against Nâzım and was going to have him knifed.

The funny thing is, the Gypsy or whoever he was who'd been lured with the promise of cash into doing the job came to see Nâzım and whispered into his ear, 'Nâzım Abi… That's the truth, but I didn't want anything to do with it, Abi. We've seen a lot of this kind of money, but it would be such a shame for my Nâzım Abi, wouldn't it?… The fool thought I was a sucker. I told him, "Idiot, go and get him yourself if you can!"'

On another occasion I was told about a more lethal plot: Nâzım was working on *Human Landscapes from my Country* in the prison garden, pacing up and down under the main wall of the prison, flailing his arms about, making short abrupt turns, muttering and mumbling…

Meanwhile, in one of the isolation cells on the top floor, three convicts in leg-irons were watching Nâzım below. They'd been put in chains and thrown into isolation because they'd killed a man three days earlier – something to do with the prison drug trade.

'That man, you see that man? His name's in history books, I swear it…'

'Of course. The man's got brains, he's educated…'

'You know what I think; I'm kind of tempted – a voice inside me says: "Kill him"… You ask me why? Well, if you're going to kill someone, you might as well kill a man like him. Look at us, what do we do? We go and take out some schmuck and then get thrown in jail for ever… But if you murder this guy, then all the newspapers in the whole world will write about you. Then your name will go down in history…'

'No,' said the third convict, 'that's our Nâzım Ağabey… How can we bring ourselves to kill him?'

I was told this by one of the destitutes who was responsible for cleaning that unit.

'Please, Kemal Ağabey, tell Nâzım Ağabey to watch out… They're completely out of their minds…'

Nâzım laughed when I told him. 'So, to make sure his name goes down in history, the guy would kill me! As if it could... as if there's nothing else he could do to get his name into the history books...'

I should mention here briefly that a few days after this incident the same three men were transferred to different prisons in Anatolia. As far as I remember, all three were stabbed to death soon after they arrived in their new jails... On hearing this news it was Nâzım who was most sorry for them. He spent a long time pacing up and down the walkway.

In the years 1941 and 1942 we suffered many gloomy, oppressive days, and nights that were even worse...

The German Blitzkrieg was in full force. Their armies were in Bulgaria, and we kept hearing that within days or even hours they'd demand right of passage through Turkey. 1942 in particular was the year when support for the Germans was all the rage in the prison. We were told there was no doubt about it: that the enemy would attack us. There was another rumour going round that a list of prisoners with sentences of five years or less had been prepared; in the event of an attack the prison would be evacuated and the prisoners sent off to Central Anatolia. The planning, we were told, was so advanced and detailed that it had already been decided who would be sent where. The relevant orders had apparently already been received...

Nâzım was saying, 'If these rampant reactionaries are successful, mankind will be set back at least a thousand years, and everything achieved so far will be lost!' Then he added: 'But the Germans will be beaten... It's a historical inevitability.'

From time to time we'd get bits of news: the Germans had entered Belgrade and carted all the young girls off in batches to the brothels.

Or that German officers drunk with victory celebrations had hanged prisoners on wires in some prison somewhere, or that Gestapo troops were doing target practice. Their target: prisoners.

Neither Nâzım nor I would get involved in that kind of talk, but it was quite clear that neither of us could get these atrocities out of our minds.

Some prisoners thought they could benefit if Hitler won, and these people started to pollute the atmosphere in the prison. One such prisoner was a 'half-caste' in one of the wards on the middle floor of the prison. He was six foot six inches tall and weighed over seventeen stone. His mother was a Tartar and his father a Turk. His childhood, his teens, in fact his whole life, apart from the last few years, was spent in Europe's major cities, mostly in Savoy. Despite this, he was always coming up with grand turns of phrase like 'the national interests of the Turkish nation'!

He was a good man, though. He was unbelievably naïve, and we were constantly amazed at how such a man could be raving about a 'Nazi victory'.

Occasionally, he would talk about 'freedom' and decent things. He could speak excellent French, German, Romanian, Serbian, Russian and Italian. He was interested in fine art, he admired Nâzım's poetry and was a rather perceptive and cultivated man. The reason he yearned for a Nazi victory despite all these 'democratic' qualities he had was, as he was always saying, that he had a lot of money tied up in a blocked account in a Romanian bank. If Germany won, he'd eventually go off to Romania and be united with his cash.

In prison, he was known as *Deve*, 'the Camel'. In the winter he was crippled by the cold and was unable to stir from his bed, so he couldn't get down to where the radio was. Though the radio was under the control of the prison administration, it was available for everyone to listen to. So the Camel would pay people to go down and listen to the news for him. He'd tip anyone who brought him 'good news' about each new German advance in Russia. Necati and Bobi Niyazi had acquired a taste for these tips... Every time there was a news broadcast, they'd make up stories about new victories and tell him that new cities had fallen to the Germans. Once they'd collected their tips, they'd come round and say, 'Come on, don't you want to share in the sucker's money?'

We'd get together in the ward where Necati and Bobi Niyazi lived. Sometimes Nâzım would join us too... Someone would make tea, and cigarette packets would be pooled. That's how we'd spend the 'sucker's money'.

There was a detailed map of Soviet Russia on the wall at the head of the Camel's bed, and he'd drawn three thick arrows in red on the map to mark the three-pronged German attack. Each day the arrows would get longer, and thanks to the efforts of Bobi and Necati, combined with his own enthusiasm (he couldn't resist making the arrows a bit longer), one of the red arrows which had stretched as far as Tula would encircle Moscow.

Nâzım would ask, 'That's all very well, Camel, I mean Your Excellency, but what if one day the German armies have to retreat and the operation has to go into reverse back into Germany?' In his broken Turkish, which he'd only recently learnt, the Camel would reply, 'Is that possible, *mon cher*, could it really be possible?'

And he'd explode with laughter.

He was yearning for the fall of Stalingrad. He promised that if Stalingrad fell, he'd treat Nâzım and me to a splendid banquet of tea and Eau de Cologne.[1]

---

1    Orhan Kemal writes in a footnote here: 'Early on in the prison it had be-

Nâzım never gave any indication of being upset by that sort of thing.

'Ah,' he'd say, 'he who laughs last laughs longest...'

Every so often we'd buy newspapers, or they'd send Nâzım some from home. If the prison administration hadn't made their clapped out radio available to the inmates and we hadn't had the papers, we wouldn't have had any link to the outside world at all. We'd just have existed in our 'box', which was unbearably hot and crawling with bedbugs in summer, and bitterly cold in winter, completely cut off from the real world.

Throughout the German Blitzkrieg, all manner of prisoners would crowd around the radio. Landowners from this or that village, wrapped in thick, warm coats with fur collars, the bare-foot destitutes of Ward 72, and between these two extremes a whole collection of individuals of various different backgrounds and ages, numbering sometimes thirty, sometimes many more than that, would crowd around the radio, their ears glued to the loudspeaker, their eyes fixed on the floor or sometimes on each other. They listened, often not understanding very much. They'd expect those who 'knew things' to explain things they'd heard to them.

Who were these people who 'knew things'? Eighty per cent – and I'm not lying – of the prison population were perfectly 'decent men' who – and again I'm not lying; I only wish I were – would cheer German successes. They were proud of German victories, behaved as if the honour of each victory belonged to our own armies, and they found comfort in that.

---

come the thing to drink Eau de Cologne instead of *rakı*. The bitterness of the Cologne would be diluted with the addition of lemon and sugar, and it was as intoxicating as *rakı*. Later on some inmates got completely plastered and attempted a belly dance in front of the chief warder. After that, Eau de Cologne was banned in the prison, like all the other prohibited substances.' (*Rakı* is Turkey's traditional aniseed-flavoured spirit, similar to *ouzo* and *'araq*.)

Foremost among them was the Camel. But the Camel would refrain from commenting in the presence of Nâzım Hikmet and me, or of the chief warder and the registrar, who shared our faith in an eventual Allied victory. So the villager and the land-owner, wherever they might be from originally, the gent from Azerbaijan or wherever, the sergeant who was a drug pusher and the thug who managed to take over the running of the prison coffee shop by instilling fear with his knife – all of them would follow the Camel, or go to his ward or that of the gent from Azerbaijan.

Necati or Bobi Niyazi would tell us what happened.

Whenever the success of the German offensives was such as to whip them into a frenzy of delight, their chests would swell with pride and they'd pile boisterously into the ward. The Azer-baijani gent, whatever his name was, would brew up a blend of the finest green or Ceylon tea, which he'd had specially brought over in yellow cellophane-wrapped boxes for his own consump-tion. The Camel would spread out boxes of chocolates, boiled sweets and Turkish Delight filled with pistachios.

Under the vacant stare of the warders who'd come in just to help themselves to tea, chocolates and sweets, the Camel would pick up his red pencil and extend the arrows representing the three-pronged attacks on his famous map. He'd go on and on, his eyes swirling, shedding copious drops of sweat in his delight and excitement.

This we were told would be followed by the expression of individual views, comments, explanations, hasty nods of ap-proval and applause emanating from hands that were as soft as a woman's, although I have to admit that calloused palms would also join in.

While all this was going on, Nâzım and I would sit in silence in our ice-cold cell, without saying anything at all, staring into each other's eyes. Nâzım would be sucking his pipe and drawing on it agitatedly, his eyes nervously darting left and right as they would when he was worried. But then, even on the blackest days, he'd suddenly blurt out, 'No way: there's no way the Allies can be defeated. History will not change its course...'

On those depressing days huddled round the radio, Nâzım drew pictures on the walls: a collection of faces, faces reminiscent of Mephistopheles, sullen and malevolent, with grotesque noses, wild staring eyes and enormous ears. Finally, after the defence of Stalingrad, when the German armies began to retreat, the Camel and his friends were thrown into a state of alarm and consternation. The Camel was completely bewildered. Anxiety and irritability took over, along with a pathetic retreat in his thinking... With the first German withdrawal he started to lose sleep, and as he lost sleep all his joy drained away, and the aches and pains in his legs intensified.

It was less crowded around the radio now, and after the news broadcasts Nâzım and I would go to the Camel's ward and follow the retreat on the map over the head of his bed. Nâzım would use a pencil to draw the new arrows going in the opposite direction. These new pencil arrows grew longer each day. The Camel would follow the retreat in abject misery and silence, his blue eyes sunk-en in their sockets in his round, stupefied face.

They all asked the Camel what the reasons were for the German retreat, as if he was responsible for the failure of the German general staff. So much so that he became the butt of jokes in the prison... They'd pull off his hat, cut out paper tails and stick them on his coat, and (pardon me for mentioning it) they'd poke his backside with their fingers.

In the end there was some talk of a 'flexible defence', a fabrication dreamt up by the so-called 'strategy experts'; this initially provided some consolation for the German-supporting big guns in the prison, but it didn't last long. It didn't last long at all, but what a load of baloney was talked right up until the moment the

German army finally surrendered unconditionally! From hidden weapons to troops supposed to be held 'in reserve' in Spain and ready for action, and much more such nonsense... Then came the conclusion we know... As the German defeat became more apparent, the Camel got progressively closer to the Allies. No doubt, with the victory, he had become as much of a 'democrat' as many of our famous Fascist writers!

*

Nâzım Hikmet enjoyed helping people around him. They'd ask him to lend them money, for instance. Most of the time, even though he didn't have any money himself, he'd go and borrow from other people and give it to whoever had asked him for help. This grew to such an extent that I remember some of the warders owing him money. But the help he gave wasn't just financial.

Most prisoners would fabricate a range of excuses in order to try and get the doctor to refer them either to the baths, or, if they had a bit of money, to the dentist or to a hospital for an X-ray. In reality this was to get some relief from the boredom and weariness of seeing the same stone walls, the concrete underground passages and iron bars of the prison, the same patch of sky, the same stretch of mountain and more or less the same faces for years on end. And it was to breathe the air outside, which for years they had forgotten. For this they needed to get permission from the doctor, or the prosecutor, or at the very least the prison governor. For most prisoners, talking to these figures of authority was way beyond their capabilities. These were 'important men', before whom one was expected to pour with sweat and to tremble and stutter. It was at such times that they would come to Nâzım for help.

'Master, explain to this doctor what I need... Tell him, so-and-so, the son of so-and-so needs a baths referral... Well, you put it as you think best... You're not ignorant like us!'

107

'All right, son, but what if he says, "Has so-and-so lost his tongue? Are you his legal representative?"'

'No, he won't – he won't say that, not to you, master. They respect you. You'll find the right words, like "He can't sleep at night", "He moans and wails", you know what to say...'

Nâzım would go off and explain the situation, talking face to face with these 'important men' and getting the permission they needed.

Once permission was granted, it was up to the gendarme on duty to let them go, but it often happened that there wouldn't be any gendarmes available in the guard room. In such situations it was usually assumed that the officer commanding the guard room was just pretending when he said, 'I haven't got any gendarmes!'

And back they'd come to Nâzım:

'For heaven's sake, master, you've done me a good turn. You might as well see it through to the end. The sergeant says "I haven't got any gendarmes!" Now it's up to you...'

Nâzım would rush out sucking on his pipe: upstairs, downstairs, through wire fences and locked doors, in and out of rooms, begging people and doing whatever he could to get what he wanted, and in the end he'd get it.

He never failed to respond to requests, such as drafting appeals or applications for legal review, or other similar tasks which would begin and end with him.

His dealings with people weren't just confined to this sort of thing. For instance, he'd give painting lessons to the regular sergeant in command of the guard room, or he'd do a pencil drawing, copied from a photograph, of the prison registrar's brother-in-law. Or he'd ignore Recep's gentle teasing when he asked questions like, 'Hey, master, where's the world heading to?'

108

Recep was a kid who was assistant to the infirmary cook. Nâzım would reply in all seriousness, giving him proper answers. Or like when the burly former wrestler who was always the butt of jokes in the prison because he was so stupid would go on at Nâzım, 'Brother, you wrote my appeal, but we didn't get anywhere with it. They upheld the original verdict... What are we going to do now?' Nâzım could have retorted by saying, 'So what? Did I charge you any money for it? You didn't even pay for the stamp on it! Shame on you!' But he wouldn't. Instead, he'd listen to the wrestler, try to console him and counsel him, not with the inner turmoil of a man crushed under the weight of a 28-year sentence compared to the wrestler's remaining six months, but as if he were enjoying his own freedom, with the light-heartedness of a man wallowing in prosperity. Meanwhile, Memiş, one of the warders, would come round in his drainpipe trousers, his spindly legs disappearing into them under his huge inflated belly. He'd ask for 'a slice of bread, if there is any...' But Memiş was a diabetic, and even a single bite-size piece would poison him. Yet, would Memiş listen?

So Nâzım would turn to him and attempt to explain at length that this tiny morsel of food could poison him. He'd try to make him understand, exhausting himself in the process – throughout which his pipe would go out and would have to be lit again several times. Finally, Memiş the warder, with supreme thick-headedness, would open wide his sunken, dull eyes and say, 'It would still be better if you gave me a slice, if there is any. I'm starving...'

Meanwhile the Camel would turn up... A discussion on the difference between the way liberalism and socialism interpret freedom would ensue, and the Camel would display an annoying inability to understand the difference...

At one point it so happened that the chief warder and his deputy both fell in love in quick succession... The chief warder with an inmate in the women's prison, and his deputy with the female warder in the same place... The women's prison was a small building in the corner of the main prison garden. When the male prisoners were let out for an airing, the women would watch the men through the cracks and knotholes in the doors, or they'd sneak into the female warder's office and look through the window there. And when the male prisoners were locked up in their wards and the women were let out for an airing, the men would watch the women through the windows of the wards... The male and female prisoners thus knew each other quite well.

As the women came out for their break, the windows of the male wards would be jam-packed with men, handkerchiefs would be waved, sighs and moans would be heard and scraps of papers would be thrown down. I never forget a rather ugly woman prisoner with very skinny legs. She had far more guts than any of the others. She'd befriended two gendarmes and no less than thirty-six of the male prisoners. We heard she was fleecing all her lovers one after the other and had thus succeeded in making a comfortable living. We heard about it because Bobi, who'd been the go-between, carrying notes backwards and forwards, and had been skilfully managing the relationships, was a friend of mine and Nâzım's as well.

One day, the chief warder's wife heard about her husband's liaison 'with a female inmate' and stormed into the prison. She went straight into her husband's office... screaming and ranting and raving. She couldn't control her rage and smashed mirrors, glasses, jugs, pitchers and window panes.

The chief warder was shaking and trembling all over. All the blood had drained from his face, which had gone a pale lemon yellow colour.

'Master, it's up to you,' he said, 'I'm finished. She heard about the affair and came over here and smashed up everything she could lay her hands on... I'm totally ruined. Go and calm her down, I beg you!'

Nâzım was, at that moment, lying down on the bed resting, his pipe in his mouth, reading an Agatha Christie novel in French. When he was tired of writing or thinking about poetry he would paint or draw, or read thrillers.

It was clear that he couldn't decide whether to laugh or cry at the chief warder's plight.

'Oh God, chief ', he said, rushing off, 'didn't I warn you?' He got back quite a while later and told us what had happened.

'With words like, "It can't be true, it must be a lie, a slur. The chief 's a good man, he's like this, he's like that…" we calmed the woman down and got her to make peace with her husband. While all this was going on, the deputy chief warder was in a world of his own, oblivious to all the turmoil, the breaking glass,

111

the noise... He was leaning against the balustrades of the stone staircase going up to the prison admin offices, his eyes fixed on the white curtained window of the female warder, and he didn't even move when I poked him in the shoulder; it was as if he was in a trance! I took him by the hand and brought him into the chief warder's office. How do you think he reacted? "What's all this?" he asked, "What's all this broken glass, why's this mirror smashed?"'

On the days when the chief warder was on leave, his deputy would invite Nâzım over in the evening. They'd have coffee and cigarettes, and the deputy would talk at some length to Nâzım about 'his love'. Sometimes I took part in these evenings as well. The crystal clear night, the brilliant moon and the huge stars did indeed make one think of love.

Nâzım's wife, Piraye Yenge, would come and visit him twice a year, or three times at the most. If she had a bit of money she'd stay at a hotel for a few days. You should have seen Nâzım then!

Piraye Yenge would phone as soon as she got off the train, or she'd come straight to the prison before checking in at the hotel. And once the necessary prison formalities were completed, she and Nâzım would sit facing each other, in either the chief warder's office or the governor's.

Nâzım had immense respect for his wife. He loved and respected her very differently from the way most ordinary husbands do. Sometimes he'd read me the letters he wrote her. These were written in prose, but they were full of poetry, plain and sincere. To read them would give you a sense of well-being and joy, and convey a love of life and a lightness of heart even when one was at the lowest ebb. One would be re-energised.

Piraye Yenge's writing style was reminiscent of Nâzım's: she was unaffected, resolute and conscious of being the wife of a 'Great Poet', someone who was aware that she possessed historic significance because of her husband, but who at the same time was proud of her own individuality.

Nâzım used to preserve her letters with great care. The ordinary, day-to-day events described in those letters provided the material for his *Human Landscapes from my Country*. Compared to his wife's sedate, controlled manner and speech, Nâzım's was, how shall I put it, impulsive and almost flippant. His speech reminded me of a nightingale's chatter. When they sat opposite each other, Yenge was controlled, commanding and serious, while Nâzım would be gesticulating, flapping his hands and arms and talking all the time. And his eyes would never leave his wife's. She would just listen, her head held high. I imagine exchanges between them might run like this:

'Look, Nâzım, you've messed up your clothes again!'

'Oh, forgive me, my love, I won't do it again!'

'If only she'd once, just once, call me "Nâzım, dearest", or address me like that in her letters, then the whole world would be mine. But she won't... wretched woman...!' he used to say to me.

It was as if his wife was a teacher and Nâzım a mischievous primary school pupil who had been rolling about in the dust, getting hot and sweaty, and had then drunk ice-cold water...

Yet listening to his wife, he was the happiest man on earth and there'd be no doubt that whatever his wife said would be the latest, most original and interesting things possible...

Around this time, I'd been going to work outside the prison. I'd leave in the morning with a number of other prisoners, and we'd return to the prison late in the afternoon or in the evening. Coming back from work one day, I saw Nâzım almost in tears, leaning against the very same iron balustrade which the deputy chief warder had leaned against while he was watching the female warder's white-curtained window.

I went up to him but he didn't even notice me. Usually he'd greet me at the door, receiving the token presents I got for him from time to time – the whistling boiled sweets,[1] the roasted chickpeas or hazelnuts, and in particular 'cigarettes from outside' – thanking me profusely. He'd be very happy, laughing and talking and listening to what I had to say about the 'outside'.

It was strange, the way he was just standing there. I knew his wife had arrived. Can you imagine? His wife comes, and Nâzım isn't elated and singing to the rafters!

I asked what had happened, but he just shrugged, sighed and turned his eyes towards the setting sun with such sadness that my heart went out to him. I asked again and again, I pressed him, I beseeched him. In the end, despite all his efforts to hide the truth, I managed to get it out of him.

Piraye Yenge had phoned as usual and told him she had checked into the hotel, was very tired and would come to the prison the following day. In the course of the conversation Nâzım said, 'The registrar here doesn't approve of that hotel. Don't stay there, move to a different hotel!'

Probably because she was tired, Piraye Yenge just dug in her heels and said, 'No. I've stayed at this hotel since I was a child (obviously with her parents) and I've never heard anything bad about it. I can't see any reason why I should change my hotel.'

'You'll change hotels.'

'No, I'm definitely staying put.'

'No, you're not…'

In short, Yenge insisted on staying where she was and Nâzım was furious.

'In that case, don't come and see me,' he said. 'Go back where you came from!'

That seemed to be all there was to it.

---

1    A type of boiled sweet with holes which whistle when you blow through them.

115

Nâzım, however, regarded this as a matter of principle, or rather a point of honour.

'I shan't speak to her as long as she stays in that hotel!'

That night he stayed up very late, making calculations, turning them over in his mind. He smoked pipe after pipe and walked around the cell, his clogs constantly clacking on the concrete floor...

Very early the following morning, Necati rushed in breathless, his eyes still sleepy, his hair all over the place.

'Master, great news: Yenge's here!'

Nâzım was in bed. He went bright red. We looked at each other. He wanted to ask me, 'What do you think?', and I wanted to tell him, 'You've got to go and see her, there's no other way!'

Necati had no idea what was going on and kept on babbling and gesticulating. On any other occasion Nâzım would have burst out laughing if he'd seen him like that...

Necati departed.

'Go and tell her,' Nâzım said, 'go and tell her to go back to her Istanbul...'

But I felt that what he really meant was: 'Don't take any notice of what I'm saying. Just deal with it, leave me alone to carry on playing hard to get for a bit.' I could see his nostrils were quivering with excitement...

I went down. As it was so early, neither the governor nor the registrar was around. And as it happens, the chief warder was on leave that day...

'Why didn't he show any interest?' Necati asked.

'I'll tell you the problem: he said: "She should go back to Istanbul. I'm not coming down."'

Necati gave a belly laugh and said, 'Wow, look at Nâzım Hikmet! Do you think he's serious?'

'Forget it,' I said. 'He's just pretending!'

In the end it was the governor who arrived first. The registrar came in immediately after him. We got Piraye Yenge inside. She smiled proudly, wearing her slightly shabby black coat. We went through the usual pleasantries. Necati found a chair for her, Bobi Niyazi seemed to be trying to work out whether he should make some sort of move to get her to give him a tip, but decided against it.

He asked Piraye Yenge if she had changed her hotel. She laughed...

The poor woman waited by herself for quite some time. Then finally, after both the governor and the registrar had pleaded with him, and after he'd played hard to get for long enough, Nâzım was ready to concede that he had been persuaded. He went down to see his wife, and not surprisingly, the ice quickly melted once they were together.

On the days she visited, Nâzım would be in a frantic state of activity from the early hours. He would have ironed his suit the previous evening, pulled his maroon shoes out from underneath the bed and got them polished, and then early in the morning he'd go down to the barber's, get his hair cut, have a really close shave and while I was still in bed, he would come and stand in front of me, immaculately dressed, ready for inspection.

'How are you? More to the point, how am I? Don't I look great?'

'Wow – you've become a second Mister Eden!'[1]

---

1    Anthony Eden was the British Foreign Secretary from 1935–1938, when he resigned in protest, it was understood, against Prime Minister Neville Chamberlain's policy of appeasement. He was again Foreign Secretary under Churchill from 1940–1945 and from 1951–1955, when Churchill was Prime Minister. He was known internationally for his stand against appeasement but also for his good looks and for dressing fastidiously. Perhaps more than any other British politician in modern history, Eden as Foreign Secretary was the quintessential well-dressed British gentleman, and it is his dress sense to which Orhan and Nâzım were referring here.

'Of course, of course, I've become Mister Eden!'

And he'd laugh, chewing on his blond moustache.

It had become the custom in our jail: parents who came to see their sons, wives who came to visit their husbands and sisters coming to see their brothers would sit facing their nearest and dearest either in a corner of the prison garden or in the visiting room. They'd eat together and talk for as long as they wanted, to try and quench the thirst of their yearning. This was all thanks to the governor. I think if I tell you that on major religious festivals he was unable to keep from crying, that will give you a fairly accurate idea of the kind of man he was...

'On this sacred, blessed day, when everyone is celebrating with his family and loved ones,' he'd cry, thinking about the deprivation we prisoners faced, 'dear God, please allow me the grace not to have to earn my living this way for the rest of my days!'

Like other prisoners, Nâzım would make the most of the governor's tolerance, and when Piraye Yenge, or his mother, or his sister and his brother-in-law came to visit, he would lay on a feast... What kind of a feast could they expect, though? Just whatever was in season and could be found in the prison grocer's: tomatoes, peppers, aubergines, okra... and one or two of the finest dishes you could cook with them.

It was again one of those religious festivals, and Piraye Yenge had come for a visit. She was there just for the day and was going back in the evening. She couldn't afford to stay the night...

As usual Nâzım was up and ready first thing in the morning, dressed in his best. He kept pacing up and down the ward, turning abruptly before he reached the end of the walkway, chewing his moustache and pulling nervously on his pipe...

At long last, word came that his wife had arrived and he went downstairs... A little later I got dressed and went down too, welcomed Piraye Yenge and then left them by themselves.

119

In the evening, after she'd left, Nâzım came up looking extremely miserable – he seemed to have aged considerably. He threw his pipe on the bed and undressed while deep in thought. He put on his red striped pyjamas, looking worn out and despondent... He leaned his head against the window overlooking the plain and gazed for a long time at the setting sun.

'Damn it,' he sighed, 'six years have gone by!'[1] Then suddenly his blue eyes sparkled and he seemed to come alive. 'Do you know what I most want at this moment? To be in Istanbul, in my own home, the home I'd have furnished with my own hands just as I'd want it to be... As evening falls, I'd take my wife and my son Memet[2] with me. We'd potter around here and there and end up in Barba-something-aki's[3] tavern, and while we'd sit opposite each other, husband and wife, drinking our *rakı*, my son would eat the snacks that come with the drinks!'

Then, seized even more vigorously by the intensity of his feeling, he said, 'For this, for this much happiness, without any hesitation I would gladly give ten years of whatever's left of my life!'

---

1   Orhan Kemal here inserts a footnote: 'The year was 1943.'
2   Memet Fuat Bengü (1926–2002) was Nâzım's stepson, Piraye's son by her first marriage. He became a distinguished writer and critic, editing some of his stepfather's poetry.
3   *Barba*, 'uncle' in Greek, became particularly associated with Greek tavern-keepers in Turkish. Nâzım here uses the expression *Barba bilmem ne-yaki*, putting *Barba* before the words meaning literally 'I don't know what' and ending it with the Greek suffix *-aki*, to indicate a Greek name.

His mother also came to visit him from time to time. Nâzım's mother was a lady with extremely fine features; she wore spectacles and her elegant, dignified manners engendered respect.

On the first day of her visits they'd chat about this and that, and then Nâzım would read her his poems. She would listen to her son intently and would often get very excited, getting into the mood of the poem.

His mother was a painter. After their private discussions – about things mothers and sons talk about – there'd be Nâzım's poetry, and then his mother would spread her paints out, set up her easel and start painting his portrait...

Meanwhile all sorts of people from the prison, ranging from the governor right down to the destitutes, would come and go, overcome by curiosity and astonished at the unusual sight of an elderly woman painting. They'd make comments and exchange views with the other people who were watching.

It was another one of those days. Nâzım's mother had arrived, dressed entirely in black. After some pleasantries Nâzım read to her at some length from *Human Landscapes from my Country*.

It had progressed considerably, and his mother listened to him visibly moved and with tears in her eyes. When he finished reading, Nâzım brought out the pictures he'd painted himself. These were portraits of various characters from the prison population. The mother, who surrendered herself almost totally while listening to her son's poetry, was not so compliant when it came to painting and kept on finding fault with her son's portraits. She criticised, for example, the way the colours were used together, and she went into various technical details about how certain colours should be grouped.

Nâzım listened to all this with his characteristic excitement and pleasure in learning something new. He made his mother repeat her advice and then put it into practice on the palette. He was pleased with the result he obtained. Then his mother sat him down in front of her and started to draw him.

She would sketch the rough outline of the model in pencil, but she would not use the pencil to embellish the outline in any way, launching straightaway into painting. Nâzım would draw a picture in pencil first. But from that day on, he gave up using the pencil, just like his mother.

Anyway, Nâzım's portrait was progressing by the minute, but don't think that he'd be sitting there motionless. He would intervene every so often to comment on his mother's work, and then he'd get told off...

'Now Nâzım dear, this is getting too much!'

'All right mother, I'm sorry... I just wanted to say...'

'You keep what you want to say for your own paintings...'

And then there'd be lots of voluble, happy, soft peals of laughter... A little later she'd turn to me for confirmation: 'Isn't that so, my son?'

Nâzım and I would look at each other.

Quietly I would say to her, 'You're quite right.'

Nâzım would look crestfallen, but that didn't stop him from interrupting again...

With many such frequent interruptions the painting would progress. Sometimes Nâzım would jump up and start explaining things, gesturing with his hands, arms and eyes. His mother would listen helplessly, holding her brushes and peering over her glasses, as if trying to say, 'Just look at him, he doesn't like my paintings!'

Her son was harsh in his judgements on anything to do with art, even where his nearest and dearest were concerned.

'Mother, dear, I didn't explain myself properly; what I meant was...' and he'd go on to explain himself at length, with his hands, his arms and the edges of his pyjamas all a flutter... As far as I can remember the argument went as follows: his mother, he maintained, chose her subjects from what was 'attractively, alluringly beautiful' and was engaged in the 'copying of beauty'. But Nâzım wanted the subject of the painting to represent not the beauty of what is generally accepted as 'beautiful', but instead the beauty of the 'ugly' that bears the impression of the social environment in which we live.

'But Nâzım, dear, what can I do? I like beauty, I can't help it!'

'Mother, I haven't explained myself clearly. What I mean to say is of course the painting of a beautiful woman is beautiful, but the portrait of Fatma Kadın who lives in a malaria-ridden village in Central Anatolia, who's just skin and bones and is extremely ugly, repulsive even, can be beautiful!'

He can't contain himself any longer and rushes to bring out a portrait which he thinks can illustrate what he's trying to say more effectively. I'm left alone with his mother. Peering at me over her glasses and lowering her voice as much as possible, she says, 'This boy's mad, just mad... It's a perfectly good picture... Why doesn't he like my pictures?'

Then Nâzım rushes in like a whirlwind, clutching the portraits he's painted.

'What I mean is, instead of just copying nature, something representing yourself...'

He talks and talks and talks.

His mother listens patiently, looking at her son over her glasses, her paint brushes in her hand...

When Nâzım got tired of poetry he'd put all his energies into painting. Anyone who could lay his hands on half a metre of canvas cloth and a small amount of white lead and glue would come and sit for him. Everyone came. The Camel, of course, and then a village landowner, the gent from Azerbaijan, one or two of the destitutes and many more...

He would first set up his easel and then open the box he'd had made especially for keeping his painting sets and spread out his paint tubes on the bed. Who cared if some of the paint tubes were split and paint got smeared all over the quilt and the blanket? He'd be eagerly whistling all along as he prepared... Then he'd start to scrutinise the face of his model. He'd screw up his eyes, then open them wide. He'd move close to his model's face, then draw back again, move close up, then draw back, sheltering his eyes with his hand as if trying to look at something in the distance, closing one eye tightly shut...

'Yes, there are wonderful colours flowing around his face.'

He would light up his pipe and enjoy a few puffs before getting down to work. Once he had an outline on the canvas, he'd lose himself in the work, trying to capture totally the meaning of the expression on the model's face, to give it some 'depth'. Often he would just throw the pipe away. The whistling would gradually get more subdued, and then at some point it would stop altogether. That would be the moment when he caught the model's 'psychological expression'. If he was satisfied with

124

the way it turned out, he'd roar 'Yes...! We've got it, my man, we've got it!'

He'd look for his pipe, but wouldn't be able to find it.

Sometimes he'd call me over.

'Come on, come and have a look,' he'd say. 'See what brave men some mothers bear...'

'You're a brave men?'

'Absolutely... Don't you think so? Surely you can't deny it?'

'Of course I don't, it's a very well deserved title...'

I'd get up from where I was sitting to see the 'psychological expression'.

'Look from this angle,' he'd say, 'here, from over here. How does it look?'

He'd be as pleased with himself as he was after writing a really forceful piece of poetry.

'Oh Lord, you don't praise me at all! Aren't I a good painter?'

Then: 'If you could brew up some tea – charge it to my account... If we could just have a few pleasurable moments in this transitory world...' That's what he'd often say, with sheer joy, delight and determination in his voice. He'd be at ease with the world, and in particular with himself, as carefree as a child.

He'd painted a few portraits of mine as well. If he'd had his way, he'd have painted more. But I found it daunting to sit for hours, my eyes fixed on the same spot, listening to his endless whistling, his constant refrain.

His models provided him, consciously or not, with a wealth of material for his epic poem *Human Landscapes from my Country*. One example was this particular individual, İbrahim, from Yayalar village. He was a good friend of mine, and of Nâzım, Ertuğrul and Emin Bey's. He resembled a wolf, with his crooked nose, bright, yellow flecked eyes and spry countenance. He possessed endless patience and would sit for hours in front of Nâzım's broken easel; sometimes from morning until midday, sometimes from midday until evening, maintaining the same pose throughout.

He barely spoke, but when he did you listened, for what he did say always had substance. We were friends for a long time and I never heard him utter anything that wasn't to the point. He was mischievous and had a great sense of humour, and he'd fire the sharpest darts of criticism at you with a sly smile on his face. He appears in one of Nâzım's poems as the character 'Yakup of Yayalar Village'. I can't remember what he was called in *Human Landscapes from my Country*.[1] He'd apparently been a soldier in the Selimiye Barracks.[2] During the First World War

---

1    The character is called Kâzım and appears in the first section of the epic. He is described as having wolf eyes and is remembering the time he was working on the railways towards the end of the First World War.

2    The Selimiye Barracks are a massive stone structure dominating the Asian

he roamed round the gardens of the barracks crushing lice under his feet,[1] and he exchanged the red cummerbund he was wearing for a Mehmet's[2] bread ration. This İbrahim from Yayalar was full of anecdotes about soldiers, particularly soldiers who had served under the Committee of Union and Progress,[3] and these furnished Nâzım with a wealth of material.

Nâzım would take notes while he listened to İbrahim, and after he'd worked on them he'd read them through to him. I'll never forget İbrahim's reaction on one occasion. 'Master,' he said, 'what you've written is far closer to what really happened than what I told you.'

---

skyline when viewed from the old city of Istanbul. It became well known in Britain when it was used to house British soldiers wounded in the Crimean War, and because it was there that Florence Nightingale led her team of British nurses to tend to them. The building is still a working barracks and is the headquarters of the Turkish First Army.

1  There is an incident described in Book 1 of *Human Landscapes from my Country* (pp. 38–9 of the Blasing and Konuk translation), where hundreds of soldiers were packed into the Selimiye Barracks in appalling conditions and infested with lice. Nâzım describes the earth in the yard of the barracks as swarming with lice which crackle and squish underfoot as you walk – 'you tread on the Mehmets' sucked blood.'

2  In Turkey, the name Mehmet is used as a generic name for Turkish soldiers, rather as a British soldier was called a 'Tommy'. In this part of *Human Landscapes from my Country*, Nâzım speaks of the barracks as 'full of Mehmets', referring to the troops of the Ottoman army. In the incident referred to here, the character Kâzım says, 'I think I killed a Mehmet one afternoon on the stone steps of the Selimiye Barracks'. The 'Mehmet' was holding bread. Kâzım wanted a slice and offered to buy it with a section of his red cummerbund. The soldier wanted the whole cummerbund. They argued, Kâzım kicked him in the groin and the soldier appeared to have died – Kâzım is left with the bread in his hand (pp. 40–41 of the Blasing and Konuk translation).

3  The Committee of Union and Progress *(İttihat ve Terakki Cemiyeti)* was originally an underground organisation that became the principal focus of opposition to the rule of Sultan Abdülhamid II (1876–1909) and spearheaded the revolution of 1908. From 1913 until 1918 the Committee was in effect the Government.

Then there was Çorbacı Memet (Memet the Soup-maker)...
This Çorbacı Memet had worked for a long time as a cook in
the prison infirmary and he was a 'Mehmet' as dignified, serious and patient as İbrahim from Yayalar. I used to sit with these
two 'Mehmets' on grey stools in the prison infirmary kitchen,
sipping tea and listening with great pleasure to their serious conversation, which was punctuated with long meaningful silences.
The Çorbacı also furnished Nâzım with a wealth of material, in
particular his recollections of events in the Kocaeli region[1] during the National Struggle.

Another character I knew from those days was an old man
who wore the medal of Sultan Reşat.[2] He was in his seventies
and dressed like a Balkan immigrant, as shrivelled and as light
as a husk, sporting a clipped white beard. He'd come to Turkey
because of the Balkan War and had ended up in prison for the
'honour killing' of his son-in-law. He bore in his heart a deep hatred of the Bulgar and the Muscovite, and in the semi-darkness
of the labyrinthine corridor of the first section[3] he would pace
slowly up and down the twenty-metre long concrete walkway.

He was perhaps the most revered of all Nâzım's friends.
Nâzım admired his self-respect, his pride, his striving not to be
a burden to anyone despite being poor and often not having
much more than one daily ration.

Nâzım often went to the old man's ward and sat on the
edge of his bed, which even though it had been patched ump-
teen times was always spotlessly clean, listening to his words of
advice. The old man's stern gaze commanded respect, and his
movements were measured and calculated. Nâzım never reacted
or responded critically to his words. He'd take notes surrepti-

---

1    The area around the city of İzmit.
2    Reşat acceded to the throne as Mehmet V in 1909. He died in 1918.
3    One of the lower areas of the prison.

tiously, and from time to time he'd gently probe the old man's memory to try and get him to recount more.

I can't remember what name this old man was given in *Human Landscapes from my Country*, but he speaks lines like these:

> There is metal which is bronze,
> there are men who are bastards,
> but then there are good ones too![1]

Then someone would have a dream. In this dream crows would land on manure and take off again...[2] All these passages in *Human Landscapes from my Country* are anecdotes Nâzım gained from his friendship with this old man from the Balkans.

The old man had no one other than his old wife, who was also in her seventies and bent double. Once a month or every other month she would come to the prison with a small bag in her hand. The old man would greet her with the asperity and vigour of his youth, his hands always clasped behind him. He would steer her along, with that domineering air which he never lost, to the shady area at the end of the prison garden. The two of them would sit there alone for hours...

Then one morning we heard that this old man from the Balkans hadn't made it through the night. He was serene in death, as if he had fallen into a soft, comfortable sleep and hadn't woken up yet. His face was very peaceful... Quite clearly he had not struggled as his life came to an end.

---

1  In *Human Landscapes from my Country*, these words are attributed to 'two red-bearded immigrants from Bulgaria' in the third-class waiting room at Haydarpaşa Station.

2  This appears in the epic as a tale narrated by one of the red-bearded immigrants: a man tells the prophet İbrahim (Abraham) that he saw crows taking off from manure to perch on branches and recite the *ezan* (the call to prayer). İbrahim tells the man that the crows are imams and hocas who dwell in manure and recite the *ezan*.

Amid the usual noise, rush and turmoil of the prison, the dead body of the man from the Balkans, his medal with its red and green ribbon on his chest, was carried on one of the special stretchers used for transferring corpses and gently placed into the hearse. Nâzım was one of the people who bore the stretcher. I was also there. The old man looked asleep... He was still a domineering figure with a frown on his clean, wrinkled face. It was as if he was carrying his hatred with him to the grave. His medal, his closed eyes, his wrinkled face, his cummerbund, his frayed red striped shirt, the white stone buttons on the narrow strip where the shirt went round his neck: everything was alive. It was just his feet... They were yellow – very yellow. Only his feet were dead...

Was there anyone who had not provided material for *Human Landscapes from my Country*? The likes of İbrahim of Yayalar, Çorbacı Mehmet, Laz Eyüp Ağa, Captain İlyas, various Balkan immigrants, the Azeri Şükrü Bey, Galip Usta...

Galip Usta... I met him after I left the prison, we became friends and I was extremely fond of him. But he's no longer the Galip Usta of old. He's a brand new Galip Usta, approaching fifty but determined to stay young. He thinks, if I had a tractor, I'd plough the fields with it, then I'd sell it for a very good price, and with the money that I'd get I'd send my children to school. Unlike me, they'd complete their education and become engineers – they'd outdo anything I've managed to achieve... He's now a young grandfather who doesn't give a thought to when he's going to die.[1]

---

1    Galip Usta is the man on the station steps 'who's famous for thinking strange thoughts' at different stages of his life. At age 10 he thought, if I could go to school; at age 15 he thought, if I could buy some yellow shoes, the girls will look at me. Nâzım ends this sequence with Galip aged 52 wondering, when will I die? Orhan Kemal is updating his 'strange thoughts' and putting them into the mouth of the real Galip Usta.

At Haydarpaşa Station[1]
Spring 1941.
      It's three in the afternoon.
On the steps: sun,
                exhaustion,
                      stress.
A man
      is standing on the steps,
            thinking about various things.

He's thin,
timid,
with a long pointed nose,
his cheeks covered with pockmarks.
The man on the steps is
           Galip Usta,
      who's famous for thinking strange thoughts.

Thus begins *Human Landscapes from my Country*.

When it came to his poetry, the most important yardstick for Nâzım was the 'people'. He used to say, 'A popular artist should first and foremost be understood by the people. He must be the people's artist.' With that in mind, he read the *Human Landscapes from my Country* many times in prison, to people of all classes. He cut out the sections he realised could not easily be understood and rewrote them in a simpler, clearer way.

People were visibly affected when Nâzım recited his poetry; some would weep, some would sigh. I was one of those who wept. There were also many who recalled their own experiences as a result of what they'd heard being read...

---

1    Haydarpaşa Station stands in a spectacular position at one side of Kadıköy Harbour on the Asian shore of Istanbul. It was built in 1909 as the terminus of the German-built railway across Anatolia that was expected eventually to run to Baghdad (see Çelik, 1986, p. 102). It came into its own, however, in the early Republican era, as it was the principal Istanbul terminus for trains both to the capital, Ankara, and to elsewhere in Anatolia. In those days it provided the only reliable means of reaching most of the country from Istanbul. It was also where Turks coming from Anatolia would first arrive in Istanbul.

'Yes, indeed Nâzım Bey, that was how they tore Ali Kemal to pieces in İzmit, and we kept on shouting "Artin Kemal"...'[1]

Sometimes Nâzım would be extremely pernickety about a single word. He'd look through various books, and in order to find the most reliable information on the origin of a word he'd go up and down stairs, rush along the corridors like a whirlwind and think nothing of waiting for half an hour or an hour just to get locked doors unlocked so that he could go from one section of the prison to the next.

He'd ask around and dig for information. He'd find elderly men among the prisoners who would be likely to know something, and he'd engage them in conversation to take them back to the old days. Finding the answer to what he'd been looking for, he'd return to the ward in a triumphant flurry.

I was to be released around the end of September 1943, and my day of release was approaching. One day when I got back from work I found a village lad – a young man – in our cell. Nâzım was explaining something to him. The lad took out a small notebook from his pocket and started to write down what Nâzım was saying: '... brushes size 1, 2 and 3, white lead, glue...'

---

1    This incident is graphically described in *Human Landscapes from my Country* (Blasing and Konuk translation, p. 75ff.). Ali Kemal was a journalist who was bitterly opposed to the Committee of Union and Progress during the First World War, not least for their treatment of the Armenians in 1915. He later opposed the nationalist movement in Anatolia. He briefly became Ottoman Minister of the Interior in 1919 and instructed the Ottoman provincial authorities to have nothing to do with Mustafa Kemal's nationalist movement. He was consequently seen as a traitor, and in 1922 he was kidnapped in Istanbul and taken to İzmit. The nationalist commander there pushed him into a hostile crowd who lynched him. Artin is a common Armenian name – the shouts of 'Artin Kemal' by the crowd in *Human Landscapes from my Country* were intended as a final insult to the man they accused of conspiring against them and of collaborating with the occupation. Ali Kemal's first wife was British, and he had lived for some years in exile in Britain.

'What else?'

'That's it for the moment.'

The lad put the notebook in his pocket. He had an intelligent, keen look.

'That's fine, master', he said, 'tomorrow's visiting day and my father should be coming from the village to see me. I'll ask him to get these for me.'

After the lad had left, Nâzım told me his story: because of a land dispute, and partly at his father's instigation, he'd killed the owner of a neighbouring field. He was sentenced to fifteen years. Using the grid square method he had been drawing enlarged versions in charcoal of photographs of various people. He'd approached Nâzım and asked, 'If I become your apprentice, would you teach me to paint in oils?' They'd come to an agreement and were going to start in the next few days. Nâzım said, 'As you can see, he's a strong lad; he's not into hashish or opium, knives or gambling.'

The lad would come every morning, sit beside Nâzım while he was painting and help him: he'd wash his brushes, squeeze paint on to his palette and prepare the canvas with white lead and glue. Then with his large eyes fixed on Nâzım's brush he would patiently watch for as long as Nâzım continued to paint. Days went by like this. I didn't know how they worked together, as I went off every morning to go to work. But Nâzım would frequently tell me about the 'really great talent' this lad[1] possessed.

It finally arrived: September 25. The next day I was to complete my sentence – I'd be released. But before that I have to tell you about the rabbit and the strawberries: I learnt a great deal more about Nâzım from these two incidents.

---

1      Orhan Kemal identifies him in a footnote here as 'The painter Balaban'. İbrahim Balaban, born in 1921, went on to become a celebrated artist.

# THE STORY OF THE RABBIT

We were working as road construction labourers in one of the outer suburbs of the city. Late one afternoon, a young boy came along with a baby rabbit, a ball of fluff with pink, syrup-coloured eyes. The boy was selling the rabbit. Everyone who was around played with the rabbit, but no one offered to buy it. I thought of Nâzım and started to bargain with the boy. We agreed on fifty kuruş and I handed over the money.

Nâzım was perched on the edge of the table next to the radio with his pipe in his mouth. Next to him was the Camel, leaning on his walking stick.

With the baby rabbit in my hand, I approached Nâzım. He was preoccupied and didn't notice anything at first, but when he caught sight of the rabbit he forgot all about the radio. He jumped up and almost snatched it from my hand!

He started firing questions at me. Meanwhile he was kissing it, stroking its fur, rubbing it against his face, putting it inside his shirt and taking it out again...

'Are you serious? Did you really bring this for me? You bought it for me? How much did you pay? Where did you buy it? Whom did you buy it from?' All the time kissing and stroking it...

'You really bought it for me? You paid fifty kuruş? Would it be rude if I reimbursed you? In that case, do forgive me... Thank you so much... You know, it's the most delightful present in the whole world...'

He walked up and down the admin block in his clogs... Then, darting into the chief warder's office, he said, 'Look, chief, look, look at my rabbit...'

Rushing out of the chief warder's office he hurried into the registry. The prisoners working there were at that moment busy with matters to do with the registration of prisoners and detainees who had just arrived from the court...

'Süleyman Bey, look at my rabbit! What do you think? And its eyes? What? Hey, Süleyman Bey, Süleyman Bey, look here...'

'Fine, master, fine, I've seen it, good luck with it...'

'Mr Clerk, here, have a look... Look at its whiskers... Mr Clerk, look at its whiskers... Look, this rabbit is more important than your files! But you couldn't care less...'

He left the Registry and disappeared down the steps leading to the workshops. After a while he rushed back:

'They all really like my rabbit... I cannot thank you enough! To think of getting it was really such a stroke of genius.'

'I see!'

'Yes, yes of course... absolutely... But my rabbit's whiskers...'

'In this case I can boast of my intelligence?'

'You can indeed, most certainly... But look at its teeth, brother... Do you know why its upper lip is split?'

'No...'

'Why not? Why don't you know? Didn't you study zoology?'

'I did, but I forgot...'

'I wouldn't have expected this from someone of your intelligence... And you know what? Not knowing that is an insult to my rabbit...'

'Is that so? Then you tell us why it's split!'

'What do they call rabbits as animals?... not the species, but collectively, what are they called?'

'*Kaadıma*,[1] perhaps? Beavers also belong to this group...'

'You do know quite a lot... What was it? *Kaadıma!* What does it mean? Rodents?'

'We're not going to forget about this business of the split upper lip! Why is it split exactly?'

'You really don't know? How come, you who know the word *kaadıma*?'

'Well, I don't know, and I want to find out...'

'You must be joking... someone who knows *kaadıma*...'

'I don't know...'

'I see, so you don't know?'

'No, I don't... but you must know, and you'll tell us!'

'Oh, all right, do you really think I know?'

'Wow!'

He laughed and chewed his moustache... and then a moment later he rushed off to the infirmary... A little later we again heard the sound of his clogs.

'You know, you couldn't have made me any happier in this mortal world...'

He roamed around, walked in circles kissing the rabbit...

'His eyes, just look at his eyes... Oh! Look at his whiskers, look at how they quiver! This creature must be hungry now, no?'

He ran off again to see the chief warder:

'Chief, chief, my dear chief, if you could just allow Bobi to go off and get a little milk...'

'Chief, should I try and get some fresh clover and feed it to it?'

'?!...'

'Look chief, look, look how it's trembling! You know, it's not trembling because it's frightened; it's frightened because it's trembling!'

---

1    Orhan Kemal cites an obscure word of Arabic origin to refer to rodents.

'!! ...'

Then off to the carpentry workshop... Begging, cajoling and badgering the carpenters. They were all mobilised, and very hurriedly a box was built for the rabbit.

I was in the cell when he arrived with the box and placed it in a corner. Somehow he'd managed to get hold of some milk, and he poured it into one of our food dishes. He put water in another dish and alongside it a couple of handfuls of fresh clover... But all in vain; the syrupy pink eyes of the baby rabbit were full of sadness... The animal was staring fixedly at one point, trembling with dread, its whiskers quivering...

Nâzım stood with his arms akimbo, observing the animal for quite some time. Then he bent down and pushed the dish of milk towards it. The rabbit jumped as if it had been prodded and turned its back on the milk. This time Nâzım pushed the clover forward, and when the animal again backed away he pushed the water forward, and again... He stood upright.

'I wonder why it's not eating. Do you know why?'

'I don't know...'

'You don't have any expertise in this area?'

'No...'

'Would Çorbacı know anything?'

He rushed out and returned with Çorbacı and İbrahim of Yayalar.

'Do you know why it's not eating?'

İbrahim was sniggering.

Çorbacı said, 'Look, master, you've overwhelmed the poor thing with all this stuff you've offered it. Leave it to its own devices and it'll eat...'

Nâzım, his fists clenched on his hips, was watching the rabbit intently. In all seriousness he remarked, 'I wonder whether this rabbit is male or female.'

138

İbrahim from Yayalar was doubled up with laughter. We were all laughing. Nâzım was chewing his moustache.

'Why do you laugh? Honestly, what are you laughing at? It's all very well for you from Yayalar village – it's just the way we are. People like us, the sons of gentlemen and pashas, that's how we are.'

İbrahim from Yayalar was still giggling. Nâzım again asked, 'Isn't there anyone here who's an expert on this?'

Eventually İbrahim says, 'Yes – Ertuğrul Bey. Get him.'

They sent for Ertuğrul. He was a man who took this sort of thing very seriously. He was an orderly in the prison infirmary and must have been busy, because his hands were wet. His brow was furrowed...

'Right,' he said. 'What is it then?'

İbrahim had gone purple in the face he was laughing so much – he had to support himself, leaning against Çorbacı's shoulder.

'It looks like you're busy, Ertuğrul... I was going to ask you something, you don't mind, do you?' Nâzım said.

Ertuğrul was still looking serious and impatient. Nâzım repeated his question: 'Were you busy?'

'Come on, man; say what you have to say, for God's sake... Yes, I'm busy!'

'Oh, I'm sorry. So you're busy?'

Ertuğrul was about to walk off, thinking they were messing him around, but İbrahim blocked the way, his face still bright red from laughing.

'Look, Ertuğrul Bey, what the master is asking is this: apparently you're an expert on this sort of thing... He wants to know whether this rabbit is male or female.'

Ertuğrul walked off muttering in exasperation while we all laughed our heads off. Finally, Çorbacı undertook the appropriate examination of the rabbit and pronounced: 'It's a male!'

139

Ah! So it's a male? In that case he needs a wife. What do you say, İbrahim, eh? What do you say to that?'

İbrahim still couldn't stop laughing.

'Come on, master. If I could, I'd get a wife for myself first...'

To cut a long story short, this rabbit became Nâzım's chief pre-occupation in the days and weeks to come. Painting and poetry were pushed aside as he concentrated his attention on the rabbit. As soon as he woke in the mornings he'd rush over to the rabbit, pick him up from his box and stroke him, and he'd often put the rabbit on his arm and go back to sleep with him. One morning he woke up and tried to say good morning with a nod of his head, looking at me with sleepy eyes.

'The rabbit', I said, 'the cat got him!'

'What!'

He shot out of bed and went straight over to the rabbit's box. The rabbit was where it always was...

'You really scared me!'

'Well, what if the cat really had got him?'

He thought for a bit.

'I swear I'd have become an enemy of the whole feline species!'

'OK, but nevertheless if...'

'Heaven forbid! Just don't say it! This is the man who gets the animal in the first place, and then he talks such nonsense...!'

he rabbit was fine, eating, drinking and roaming around the cell as he pleased. One morning Nâzım put him in Ertuğrul's bed. Ertuğrul didn't just dislike the animal, it infuriated him... I sneaked along and called Ertuğrul over to have a look. He came over and saw that the animal really was in his bed.

'What right do you have, sir, to put the animal in my bed?'

'Why shouldn't I?' said Nâzım.

'It will pee, it's filthy!'

140

'It's your bed which is filthy... See,' he sniffed it. 'Yuk!'
'I'll kill your bloody rabbit one of these days...'
'You dare!'
'All right, you'll see! You'll find him dead one morning!'
'In that case, Ertuğrul, I'll strangle you!'

In the end, Piraye Yenge came and took the rabbit away with her, and Nâzım and the rest of us were thus freed of it... Nâzım went back to his painting and his poems.

# THE STORY OF THE STRAWBERRIES

※

It was the strawberry season and someone had given Nâzım a punnet of strawberries as a present. They were really big, ripe, juicy, wonderfully gorgeous... Nâzım clutched the box to his bosom; his face as red as the strawberries, his blue eyes sparkling with pleasure.

'Wait,' he said, 'let's get some icing sugar, and then...'

We ordered icing sugar through one of the warders. Until it arrived we picked off one by one the tiny green leaves forming the caps of the strawberries. All the while, Nâzım was reciting odes to the strawberry, heaping praise on the fruit.

'You know what we'll do next; one layer of strawberries, one layer of sugar, one layer of strawberries, one layer of sugar... Then we'll get our spoons and...'

Our mouths were watering as we picked the caps off the strawberries. And when the icing sugar arrived, we put one layer of strawberries, one layer of sugar, one layer of strawberries, one layer of sugar... Everything was ready. But just as we grabbed our spoons and were about to launch into the fray, Nâzım was summoned to go to the admin office!

'Oh, to hell with it! Once in a blue moon we get to enjoy the pleasure of eating strawberries!'

He got up to go, but gave a strict warning: 'Look here, no cheating! You are not to eat any until I get back...'

'I swear I'll try not to,' I said, 'but what if I can't help it?'

'Don't even think about it! You'll make me commit murder for the first time in my life!'

I burst out laughing. He rushed off and not long afterwards he rushed back in.

'Now,' he said, 'even if someone says "Your father Hikmet Bey has come back from his grave," not even then am I going to let go of these strawberries!'

We attacked them from opposite sides. We ate and ate so many that finally, even though there were still a few left on the plate, we just fell back on our beds, sated.

'Ah,' said Nâzım, 'at least I shan't be saying I haven't had my fill of strawberries.'

The bitter-sweet memories of the three and a half years of prison friendship I shared with Nâzım Hikmet are not of course confined to the anecdotes I have recorded here. But relying only on my memory alone, this is all I can now recollect.

I had notebooks in which I wrote on a daily basis his most typical moments, notebooks in which I'd recorded enough documentary material to write a massive book about him... But I no longer have them.

I have squeezed my brains to the last drop, like a lemon, to try and recall more, and I am very well aware that I have not been able to write about Nâzım Hikmet as much as he deserves.

It was our last night together. The following day, after five years in jail, I was going to be released early in the morning and be united at last with my freedom. I suddenly felt inspired to write poetry. It really struck me that I was going to leave him behind in prison and I was gripped with that feeling you have when you leave your father or mother, your brother or sister or your own children, that wrenching feeling. I scribbled down a few lines. Just as I'd finished, he walked into our cell, holding the copper mug from which he always drank his tea. He was looking for something on the shelves and was about to dash out again when I thrust my poems into his hand. He took them and read them.

*Funny Freedom*

Yes
It means
it means in three days time
Yes
what you call
                'Funny and sweet
                      FREEDOM!'
'My dearest friend
my master!'
The concrete, the iron bars, the dusty light bulbs, leaving these to
                  some others!

Yes
this freedom,
the bell, the clink of the lock, the warders
the yearning to leave these behind!
But
to look at you from beneath the blue sky
to leave you behind in prison!
Me in a different kind of prison
without iron bars, without locks,
without dust on the light bulbs
and without warders.

Yes
the freedom you mention is
FUN-NY!

Trains come and go
You can let your shadow fall on whichever street you like...
What freedom?
Come on my friend
my dearest dear master.

*

*To Nâzım Hikmet*

You,
'The man who stuffs the screams of Prometheus
into his pipe as if they were coarse-cut tobacco'.
You, my blue-eyed friend,
there's no way I'll forget you.

September 26, 1943.
Leaving you all alone in prison
sailing before the wind in a third-class compartment
I shall rush to my hometown.
And the train
will enter the station in a flutter like a pigeon,
to a tearful young woman
after five years
it will bring her husband.

At that moment – ignoring those at the station –
kissing my beloved on her cheeks
you'll look at me with your joyful eyes
from within me.

At that moment when everything will be banished from the heart
BREAD – ENMITY – LONGING
but Nâzım HİKMET,
although you are so many kilometres away
resting your blond head on the walls of my enlightened heart
you'll make your friend cry with the sadness of a setting summer
  sun.

Days will go by.
I shall be immersed in the struggle to earn a living.
The factory.
The machinery.
My bench.
I'll send you sugarbeet and oranges.
My wife will knit woollen socks.
Each week we'll write letters
– provided I get no call-up to the army.

How can I forget you?
The prison nights when we'd pick out the bedbugs
and the curse of the horrific moments
while we waited by the radio for news from the eastern front!
– on the wall by the radio
you'd drawn pencil sketches of grim human faces –

How can I forget you?
I can still hear on the concrete walkways
the clatter of your wooden clogs!

How can I ever forget you?
From you I learnt how to love the world and our people,
writing poetry and short stories
and fighting like a man, all these I learnt from you!

He looked at me, he read them again, then he put the mug aside, smiled at me with his tear-filled eyes and embraced me.

'Thank you,' he said, 'thank you! Nothing could have made me happier!'

*

And on the morning of September 26, 1943, which had started with brilliant sunshine, I embraced him repeatedly and bade him farewell under the yearning gaze of my other prisoner friends. Leaving him at the prison gates, I took my suitcase in my hand and went outside…

Happy as I was to be reunited with my house, my hometown and my five-year-old daughter whom I'd left behind when she was only forty days old, I was immensely sad to be separated from Nâzım – it was a friendship which knew no bounds.

The roads: roads filled with dust and the sun…

Before me I could see him and all the others… Especially the others… They were sad and looked almost resentful, as if it was my fault they were staying inside.

'Well, your trials are over!'

'You've got through those five years like anything, you bastard!'

'Your head will reach the clouds now!'

'Have a glass for me too, OK?'

\*

Only Nâzım, no one else, knew, could possibly know, that I was leaving a huge chunk of my heart in jail, and that I was bringing home the friendship of those still in prison.

*Adana, 1947*

# ORHAN KEMAL'S PRISON
# NOTES

※

## 19.5.1942. Tuesday

It is a murky day. It is drizzling. It is cold. We could not go to
work. 'The rain, they say, is gold,' said Nâzım. Then he took
out the wilting flowers that were on the table. He changed the
water. And he was singing as he put the fresher ones back in the
jar. I asked: 'Are you singing to the flowers?' 'Yes,' he said, 'my
flowers are used to singing. They grew up with songs.'

We drank some milk. We chatted about scouting. Nâzım
Hikmet was still busy with the flower arranging. Ertuğrul told
us his grandmother used to say, 'Oh, I feel so cheered up,' when
she saw the scouts drilling in Istanbul Lisesi.[1] Nâzım Hikmet
said, 'Looks like your grandma was quite a lecherous old hag.'
Ertuğrul objected. Nâzım Hikmet objected to the objection.

---

1    This is a secondary school. Its origins date back to 1884, but it started
     to use the name İstanbul Lisesi in 1910. This was the first time the term
     *lycée* (*lise* in Turkish) was used in Turkish for an educational institution.
     İstanbul Lisesi has a long tradition of scouting.

And saying, 'We've rearranged the flowers,' he got up. He did an about-turn and looked as if he did not know what to do next. Eventually he sat down on his bed. 'Let's have some order round here now,' he said and started to straighten his bed. He was working and talking at the same time: 'Yesterday I told Ala-eddin Bey how we were sponging off the workers. He was very upset. 'Don't let them know about this,' he said.

## 21.5.1942

Off to work in the morning... I got back blind drunk in the evening. I am now in our room with Nâzım Hikmet. I quote:

'Now whatever next! Aah! Looks like we've got extra cash here. I wonder if I took too much from someone?'

Some objects carved in wood have arrived from his friend in Sinop. Nâzım Hikmet ensures these things are sold. I laugh at his inability to balance the ten liras and a bit, despite his being a doctor of economics. Akif the Albanian turned up. The master wants to sell him an automatic cigarette box. All the salespeople I know have to serve their customers with a smile on their faces, but our friend thinks nothing of insulting them, and then admonishes them and lectures them.

'For God's sake (turning to me), work this out for me. How come I get 45 kuruş extra out of 14 liras? Please stop writing.' Then he talks to Marmara Şakir:

'Two sewing boxes make 310. OK, Marmara? That's a stiff price all right. Oh, stop, don't bother any more. We'll do the rest.'

## 22.5.1942

Evening. We have returned to the prison from our work place. Nâzım Hikmet was in the middle of some financial transaction involving Necati and the Grocer, who had been a captain in the army. Nâzım was adding up figures on the walls. He finished his calculations and went into the kitchen. We are now going to have dinner. Our meal is mushy rice. It is rather like *bulgur*,[1] the kind of food which makes you say, 'We thank God for this and may we not be in need of it!' We got up from dinner. Nâzım Hikmet looked rather sullen. I asked him the reason. 'I worked in the carpentry workshop today. I'm very tired,' he said. This look does not suit him at all. Or perhaps that is how I see it, probably because we have got used to his being cheerful all the time. If he has a good sleep tonight he should be all right. I think he has gone down to listen to the radio.

## 23.5.1942

Night time... Outside a frog has come out from nowhere. It keeps on croaking 'Ribbit, ribbit, ribbit.' The damned thing makes such an awful noise. As if it were being strangled. Nâzım is also irritated by this:

'The bugger thinks he's a bird!' he says. 'There can't be many animals which rate themselves so highly...'

Just at that moment – Almighty God seems to have nothing to do tonight – the creature starts croaking even louder. 'Listen,' says Nâzım, 'it's as if it heard us.'

## 24.5.1942

Morning. Nâzım Hikmet picked up the box he had been working on in the carpentry workshop. He proudly shows it to us. His character is such that he never boasts about anything he is really an expert on. However, when it comes to an area where he

---

1  Boiled wheat.

is not the master of the craft but an apprentice, God help us! For instance, of poetry he says he is really new to it, that his ambition is to become a good writer, etc. On the other hand, for example, he brags about being a tremendous carpenter. The justification for this is the famous box.

## 25.5.1942

I woke up at six this morning. I got up. I had to look for a safety pin in the suitcase. The lid creaked just a little. I think I woke up Nâzım Hikmet yet again. He sulked. He looked at me miserably from underneath his quilt. Then he hurled himself out of bed in a fury. He put on his socks. He picked up his famous rubber-soled shoes. Speaking of rubber-soled shoes: this year, a slight alteration has been made to these shoes he bought for five liras last year: using the paper puncher in the admin's office, he made holes in the canvas sections of these shoes. They are supposed to be airholes. I asked him about these as we were strolling round the garden yesterday, and he gave me a long lecture on the benefits of holes.

His trousers are linen. Our room is totally silent apart from the ticking of our small Japanese clock. Nâzım Hikmet furiously pulled on these linen trousers, making a rustling sound. He grabbed his jacket. He picked up the pen, the notebook, the leather cigarette pouch and the like which were his, but were on my wooden chest. Then he bent down and looked at the clock. He went out. Where to, I don't know. I think maybe downstairs, to where the radio is.

Well, this is the way of the world. Last night I had gone to bed. He and Eyüp Ağa were playing backgammon. I was impossibly sleepy. Just as I was falling asleep, I was woken up by the clacking sounds of the backgammon, and of course it was rather difficult to go back to sleep.

But the master had not gone down to the radio. He got someone to boil some milk and sent me a glass too. He wants me to know that he understands that when I woke him up I had no malicious intention. In any case, he has always been forgiving to those who have done him wnong.

## 2.6.1942

Evening. Nâzım Hikmet is now listening to the platitudes of Nurettin Artam[1] on *Radyo Gazetesi*. As there is a lot of interference on the radio he keeps on turning off our electricity supply at the mains downstairs.

Nâzım Hikmet is back. At the door of the infirmary he is shouting: 'Come on, open up. Look, I've done it again.'

What he has achieved is to lay his hands on half a lemon...

As usual, he enters the room in a flap. His entry into a room is famous – and quite something. He bursts through the door like a whirlwind: newspapers, papers, books, jacket, waistcoat, everything goes flying.

Anyway, he came in.

'Our master is quite something, really quite something,' he said. That remark was aimed at me. I'd just washed my feet and I realised that I had inadvertently put my right foot on top of the table where a bowl of lettuce was standing. I was busy writing in my notebook, resting it on my right leg. I removed my foot immediately, of course.

---

1    Nurettin Artam (1900–1958) was a writer and broadcaster who, for nearly ten years, presented *Radyo Gazetesi* ('Radio Newpaper'), a 15-minute daily round-up of Turkish and international news broadcast on Ankara Radio.

Nâzım Hikmet is really flustered. He is grilling fish. The cherries, as juicy and crunchy as black grapes, had been left in the pan.[1] Our menu is quite exceptional tonight. It would compare favourably with Europe.

'Is Kâzım Bey here, Kâzım Bey or Ertuğrul?'

On the infirmary walkway Nâzım is again like a whirlwind. Who knows why he is looking for them. The lights in the infirmary are constantly being switched on and off. From the iron door of the infirmary Nâzım shouts with all the strength he has:

'This was on, you have turned it off again, you see! Come on, it was on where we are, and you turned it off yet again!'

He came rushing into the room. He picked up Ahmet Rasim's novel *Tecarib-i Hayat*,[2] although the novel was completely innocent of any wrong doing, and then put it back down again. I really could not make head nor tail of what he was up to.

He left the room muttering, 'Come on, open the door, lad, for God's sake.' He almost flew down the stairs. He is shouting at the supervisors. I can hear his voice.

By the infirmary door he is now explaining things about electricity to the electrician. The man must be quite stupid for I can hear Nâzım's voice rising: 'Open up!'

The door is opened and Nâzım Hikmet comes down. He has a fork in his hand as he was cooking fish in the kitchen when the racket started. He rushes in.

'You take out that fuse to start with!'

Who knows what order he gave to whom.

'Has it come on now?'

I answered: 'Yes, it has.'

'Which side?'

---

1    There weren't enough bowls and plates in the prison, so cooking pans were used as fruit bowls.

2    *Experience of Life.* Ahmet Rasim (1865–1932) was a prolific writer, journalist and translator.

Someone somewhere replied...

Nâzım Hikmet uttered a 'Phew!' coming into the room, picked up something from the shelf and went out again. This went on until lunchtime.

## 13.6.1942

It's five in the afternoon. It's very hot. Nâzım Hikmet is sitting on his bed, drawing a tulip on a stone he is holding in his hand. He is looking around for a rubber eraser.

'Have you got a rubber?'

There was one on my case. Nâzım said 'Here it is!' and picked it up.

'Sir,' I said, 'are you going to waste our rubber by rubbing stones?'

He laughed. 'I've never seen a man who exaggerates as much as you do,' he said.

He started rubbing out the tulip on the stone. I chuckled.

'Come on, why do you make fun of my tulip?' he asked.

A little later he got up and started looking for something on the shelf.

'Where are those Turkish designs? There was a history book here. It should be here.'

I laughed. At that moment I was starting to put these notes together. 'Stop,' I said, 'can you repeat this slowly, so that I can note it down?'

His lips were quivering as he was forcing himself not to laugh: 'Look, at least you could do it without telling me, so that I can behave normally. Otherwise I won't even be able to move.'

While Nâzım Hikmet was painting his tulip on the stone using paint his mother gave him (we had learnt it was called *gouache*), I observed him constantly. He is wearing a sleeveless vest and red striped pyjama trousers. His lower lip protrudes as he paints the tulip on the stone. He cleans his brush on the grass-filled mattress. He whistles. One thing that is typical of him, or rather not one but two things: he always whistles when he paints. In fact, if you listen carefully to his whistling you can easily gauge the tempo at which he is painting. For example, when he is working with his brush over a section of the painting which does not have any particular importance, then the whistling is fast and regular. When he is painting the more delicate sections of the work, his whistling becomes slower and softer. The second thing he does that is typical is to close one eye and move the picture backwards and forwards, scrutinising it all the time as he does so.

The stone on which Nâzım Hikmet was painting the tulip had been found by Marmara Şevki and me in the Deli stream near Kestel.[1] The picture of the tulip is progressing.

Memet from Bulgaria walks into the room:

'Master, the news on the radio is almost over.'

The master puts down the stone he is holding:

'Is it really? Why didn't you tell me then?'

He runs to the infirmary door:

'Open up, open up!'

The door is opened. Now we can hear the radio from downstairs.


## 9.2.1943

This morning I was woken by the voice of the deputy chief warder, Basri Efendi, talking loudly on the infirmary walkway:

'Hasan has died as well.'

Since yesterday, that is within a time frame of eighteen hours, this is the third victim among the destitutes. One of the dead

---

1    A village outside Bursa.

158

was taken away yesterday in the rubbish cart. The second one is in the pharmacy next to our room.

Hasan was insane. He was one of the inmates of Ward 72.

Destitution: we have become so inured to it that when in the morning I saw the corpse, which was just a bag of bones and as light as a feather, I could feel no compassion, only disgust. I remember him well; I often used to see him rummaging in the rubbish dump next to the massive iron gates of the prison. He had a thin yellow face, and had sewn bits of coloured rag, buttons and pieces of tin on to the collar and front of his jacket, which was literally falling apart. He had done the same with his cap. They used to make fun of him, calling him 'the Marshal'.

It was midnight. I was dozing, trying to fall asleep, when Nâzım Hikmet poked my leg with his hand:

'Wake up: Kursk has fallen, Kursk.'

I came to immediately: I was delighted. Nâzım Hikmet had brought the radio into our room. He had turned the volume right down; it was broadcasting the Soviet extraordinary communiqué. Nâzım Hikmet is like quicksilver, darting all over the place, his blond hair all tousled, his eyes sparkling with glee.

'Wow, so Kursk has fallen.'

'Kursk has fallen, that's quite something! This is it.'

'It'll be Kharkov tomorrow, and then Rostov, and then...'

He woke up Ertuğrul:

'Ertuğrul, Ertuğrul, psst, Kursk has fallen.'

Befuddled by sleep, Ertuğrul replied, 'I heard.'

Then Nâzım Hikmet took the radio downstairs and went to Alaeddin Bey's ward.

He does this every evening in any case; after listening to the Soviet communiqué and finding out which cities have fallen back into Soviet hands he rushes into Alaeddin Bey's ward. There is a detailed map there and he finds the recaptured cities on the map.

For Nâzım this is probably just a very normal reaction, and he has no malicious or spiteful intent. But our esteemed Alaeddin, the Camel, swears like anything. He has also been heard to say: 'Nâzım Hikmet keeps on waking me up at midnight. When the Germans eventually start their summer offensive, then I'll be waking him up.'

He is a stupid hulk of a man, this Camel. What he is saying is a fantasy. But just in case, should he do anything of the sort and wake me up, I shall be ready to hurl the table and the charcoal brazier at him.

### 10.2.1943. Wednesday

It is snowing. Both Nâzım Hikmet and I woke up well after 10 o'clock. The Soviets released another official communiqué last night. We listened to that, and then I read for a bit and after that went to bed. I woke up in the middle of the night with the sound of loud conversation coming from the infirmary. This talking, noise and commotion went on for quite some time. At one point the door of our room opened. Two people came in. It wasn't clear who they were, as the room was dark. Nâzım Hikmet jumped out of bed, shouting. The two who had come in identified themselves. They were Ertuğrul and Recep. Then they told us what had happened: Nuri, an orderly in the infirmary, had gone berserk.

### 17.2.1943. Wednesday

Deaths follow in quick succession. Two more old men have also gone. One of them is Ali Baba, the other Emin Dede. Ali Baba was short and with his white glasses reminded you of the olds-tyle petition writers we used to have. He was a quiet man, totally shrivelled up, minding his own business, extremely mean, but quite likeable. He had fifteen more years of his sentence left, so you could say that death was a release for him. Emin Dede was an interesting character. The lines like 'I saw crows...' and 'There is metal which is bronze, there are men who are bastards', which Nâzım Hikmet used in *Human Landscapes from my Country* were taken from this Emin Dede.

He was totally worn out and was in a pitiful state. He was a fervent Muslim, a Muslim of the really extreme kind. We had gone to work together on the same shift quite a few times. On his chest he wore a copper medal with a red ribbon. He never neglected to pin it on to his dirty, patched striped shirt. The only thing he was proud of in this world was this medal. I think he had received it during the Balkan War, but it might have been older than that. How would this deeply religious man react if he knew that he was being buried without being washed?

A smallpox epidemic was raging. The first vaccinations we had did not produce the desired result, so Nâzım Hikmet was vaccinated again the following day. I have been neglecting getting this done. I have no intention of dying like Ali Baba, Emin Dede and a host of others. I love the world and believe that I have a lot to do on this earth.

It is now morning. Last night Nâzım Hikmet brought the good news that Kharkov had been taken. He is asleep now, or perhaps not asleep but just daydreaming with his eyes shut under the quilt. As of tomorrow, we are to stop eating together. On his insistence. If he gets his budget balanced in a month or two, he said, we shall revert to eating together. 'I have to sustain myself on ten liras a month,' he said – as if I could afford anything more.

### 5.4.1943. Monday

Last night I dreamt about my wife. No, I did not see her exactly, but the dream was about her. It was like this: I had been released and gone to Adana. I arrived home exhausted. After I washed and change, I lay down on the divan. My sisters were now grown up; they gathered round me and asked all sorts of questions about my five years in jail. Suddenly I remembered; where is my wife, where is my daughter?

My mother said, 'They are in Hotel Altan, your father insisted on that.' Oh my God... I got really worried. I didn't know where to direct my anger. A thousand thoughts raced through my mind. A twenty-year-old woman staying all alone in a dubious place like a hotel... I got up from the divan like a madman. I tried to put on my clothes as quickly as I could, with all the agility I could muster. But no way! It's one of those nightmares where you try to escape, but you get heavier and cannot move. Despite all my efforts, I seemed to be dressing so slowly, and I became frantic because of this... At last I managed to put on my trousers, grab my jacket and was about to leave the house when I woke up. Thus I missed out on seeing my wife, even in my dream. We live in such a world that a man cannot see his wife in his dream, let alone in real life.

The morning got off to a very grey, leaden start. It is freezing cold. I am so upset that it will be quite something if I do not quarrel with someone... Nâzım Hikmet has started off again with Tolstoy's *War and Peace* with Emin Bey from Sarıyer. I am having my coffee out of a tea glass filled to the brim and am about to light up the best cigarette I can find. I am still angry.

Nâzım Hikmet's appetite is really good these days. He is back from breakfast. He has so much hair – blond and curly. Round his neck he has tied a light green handkerchief, a product of his own weaving workshop. He is wearing the fur-collared overcoat which makes him look like HRH Prince someone or other. He is sitting at his thirty-year-old outdated typewriter, the one with the Chicago trademark, and Emin Bey is reading the drafts of the Tolstoy translation. Nâzım Hikmet is typing at a speed that does not look like a novice's. In fact, he is typing with commendable speed. Before this typing session we had the following conversation. I asked him a strange question; I cannot remember it now. And he replied – oh, yes, I remember my question – I asked him the meaning of a word in French: *limaçon.*[1]

'Well, I honestly don't know,' he said. 'As you know, as far as fish are concerned, I am very good at differentiating between a whale and an anchovy.'

We had a good laugh, and started a bit of verbal horseplay. He continued: 'When it comes to trees, I get confused between the maple, the ash and the cypress. I am very familiar with the poplar, the willow and the pine…'

He says everything in such a strange way that I can honestly say that it is rather as if honey trickles from every word he utters. This man is not just a poet. In terms of his function in life, or even physiologically, he is 'a machine that produces poetry'. This poetry 'substance', which is as rare in people as honey is in carob, he has by the kilo or even by the ton. And, how can I put it, Nâzım Hikmet is like a honeycomb, the wax of the comb is too flimsy, and the honey, the poetry, oozes out so abundantly, is so gooey! I am not writing this as a compliment to him: I write it despite myself. The relationship between us is not just that between 'master and apprentice'. We quarrel from time to time, speak rather harshly to each other, and we do not talk for days. We get angry with each other. That is to say, just as one argues, quarrels with ordinary people and stops talking to one another, Nâzım and I, from time to time, do all of these things. I'll go further and confess something: the feelings of jealousy and being full of oneself, these feelings which are present in everyone's make-up, overtly or covertly: I admit I frequently had such feelings towards

---

1   The word means 'snail' and 'cochlea', the spiral cavity of the inner ear.

others. But I never could feel like that towards Nâzım, even at the height of my anger towards him. For me, he was always this enigmatic, unreachable, larger-than-life poetry machine.

I do not know why I am writing all this. But I know this for sure: I love him very much. Quite differently from the way I'd love a brother, a teacher or, I don't know, a master or something. I feel in me a huge avalanche of love towards him in which the kind of love I have for my father, my mother, my sisters and my daughter is all interwoven. And although we do not know which one of us will depart this world first, I think of the day I will hear of his death; where that will be, how it will be. What shall I do when I am faced with the news of his death? I think of his death as being like that of Abdülhak Hamid.[1] I often have these feelings for those I love dearly.

In short, I love Nâzım Hikmet so much that sometimes I get mad at him for 'being a good man, a great figure and an outstanding person who is beyond one's reach'. I should also add the following:

Sometimes he appears to be so impervious that I become consumed with anger and run away. For example, in the prison there is a group of people we come up against all the time. They are the tie-wearing pseudo-gentlemen: the accountant, the cashier – I deliberately say cashier as an insult, rather than treasurer – the clerk, the debt collector, this kind of petit bourgeois. Their character is quite transparent: their presumption lacks any justification. Signs of gross self-satisfaction seem to ooze from their every action and utterance. One of them, for example, says to Nâzım:

'Look here, Nâzım,' (they call him by his name, without using any kind of courtesy title or form of address like 'master' or 'Nâzım Bey'. They themselves really value these epithets and

---

1    The poet Abdülhak Hamid Tarhan (1851–1937).

insist on their being used with their own names when they are addressed. In fact, they quickly become offended and angry if you fail to address them in this way. In that case they hold a grudge against you and speak ill of you behind your back) 'Look here, Nâzım, you don't understand people. You're not a good judge of character.'

When they say such things, these people do not consider for one moment that they are addressing a man who is a great poet, dramatist, political writer, scriptwriter, short story writer and novelist: in short, someone who has received the accolade of 'the engineer of souls', not through the diplomas of this or that university, but through what the older generation call 'the gift of God', his own talent. While I would be fuming at this, Nâzım Hikmet would show not the slightest anger towards the bum who said to him, 'You're not a good judge of character.' Nâzım would just smile at him and look at him vacantly. I know how meaningless and vacant that look can be, but it would speak only to those who have the intelligence to comprehend it. When Nâzım looks vacant like that – and who knows what he is thinking – he really knows this stupid man inside-out and reads him like a book. He has seen millions of people like him. He knows him in the way he knows himself, as if he is looking in the mirror.

What infuriates me is this disconnected attitude of Nâzım. For a second I want him to get angry at the man who says, 'You're not a good judge of character,' and I want him to rant and rave and tell him off. I even consider doing that myself, but then I think if anything needs to be said, Nâzım Hikmet would be a better judge of how to react. He is not a man who is unable to defend himself, so I cannot act as his defence counsel. If needs be, I can help him in some other way. So despite the pressure of my instincts, I get up in a furious rage, start swearing and leave the scene. No one really understands whom I am swearing at or why I am swearing.

Let's get back to where we were. Nâzım Hikmet continued:

'I can also identify the chestnut tree, but only after the tree has produced chestnuts... As for flowers, I know the rose and the daisy.'

Emin Bey asked: 'What about basil?'

He responded like a dynamo generating poetry: 'Basil? This is the first time I've heard of anything so ridiculous.'

While we are talking, I write down what he says on the back of my cigarette packet, in my notebooks, wherever there is space, then I put it in my diary. He is now typing like mad. And I am going to write a letter to my wife.

## 6.4.1943

Night-time. Nâzım Hikmet is sitting at his typewriter. He is going to write a letter to his wife. As he puts the paper in the typewriter, he says to me:

'You know what I like best of all the things you wrote about me?' (I had just read to him what I wrote above.)

'What?'

'My expert typing. I so much wanted it to be appreciated...'

What can you do but laugh? I told you, this man is just quite something.

# LETTERS FROM NÂZIM HİKMET TO ORHAN KEMAL

✳

## June 1944

Raşit, my brother,
I read your letter twice with great pleasure. And I shall read it
again. Your notes were excellent. The poems were also good.
Just one thing, in such short poems describing a state of mind,
in these off-the-cuff verses, there should – in my view – be good
rhyming. As you say, poetry is indeed an adroit and masterly way
of expressing oneself.

But what made me read your letter twice over, and what is
going to make me read it again twice over is what you have written about my dearest granddaughter, Yıldız.[1] In my mind's eye
she is so full of life, and I am so fond of her that I cried when
you described how she came to you to complain when she got
a beating from her mother. Do please tell my daughter that if
she beats Yıldız again I swear I shall cross swords with her. You

---

1  The child in question is Orhan Kemal's eldest daughter, Yıldız. Nâzım
   Hikmet is referring to her as his grandchild to indicate the closeness
   he feels for the parents and the child. He refers to Orhan's wife as 'my
   daughter'.

169

could not beat such an adorable and intelligent creature even if she were a cat, let alone my precious Yıldız.

Look, Raşit, I have a request of you and my daughter; I am rather embarrassed to say it and forgive me for it, and I must tell you right from the start that if it becomes impossible for any reason whatsoever I shall not take offence; the point is, if the new child you are expecting turns out to be a boy, name him Nâzım. But as I said, if you have already made a promise regarding this, or if there are other obligations, I shall withdraw my request. But if there are no objections or impediments to my name being given to your and my daughter's son, it will make me inordinately happy.

The large and small boxes for my daughter and granddaughter have been sent from Sinop. And I sent them to your father through the relatives of our Şakir Ağa from Mersin. They came to visit him and know your father. You will get them from him and then let me know. I sent you twenty liras about a week ago. Have you received it? If you can be patient a little while longer, I shall be sending you thirty or forty liras towards the end of the month. Your loom will have started working normally.

I have another request of you. In my *Landscapes* there is a labourer called Fuat. According to the plot he is to be released and should go to Adana to work as a fitter. Put yourself in his place, and in your letters to me write a few things in his words about his circle and his friends. I shall work on them and use them in the *Landscapes*. This way something, albeit short, from the workers' environment in a southern city will be included in the book.

I got a letter from Sabahattin too.[1] What he said to you about me he is now telling me to my face. This time I was really embarrassed.

---

[1]    Sabahattin Ali (1907–1948), a prominent left-wing writer and poet who was also imprisoned as a result of his political views. He was believed to have been murdered in an unsuccessful attempt to leave Turkey illegally to go to Bulgaria, after he had been refused a passport.

For the last two or three days, no longer than the last three days, I went through a short period of laziness. Tomorrow, I shall start working again.

You may remember the artist İbrahim the Barber who is here. His painting has improved immeasurably, phenomenally. I am very proud of this, and I tearfully brag with joy about this development which is just an example of the great talent possessed by our people.

This great nation of Turks! How creative it is, like all the peoples of the world, and how it deserves admiration; to die for it is the least important thing. One has to work, to live and to work, and to fight.

I had a letter from Sülker.[1] I replied, but have not received a reply to my reply.

I embrace you. No, I shall not start with you, and I am not starting with my daughter, in fact I am cross with her. I embrace my granddaughter, you and my daughter with longing. Do not leave me without letters. The three of you are right in my heart. Now, soon there will be four of you. Just take care: giving birth can be quite a dangerous thing.

Nâzım

## 1946

Raşit, my brother,

My late reply to your delayed letter is not retaliation. It is just that I was ill: a slight chill. It is over now and I am well. Firstly, the waterproof rubber sheet for my future grandchild could not

---

1    Kemal Sülker (1919–1995), journalist, writer and trade unionist who subsequently played a major role in the trade union movement in Turkey and in left-wing politics. He wrote a biography of Nâzım Hikmet and several books about his work.

be found here either. I ordered it from Istanbul. I have also asked the doctor. If he can find it in the hospital or at the place where the hospital gets it from, he will buy it for me. I think I should be able to send you the waterproof sheet soon. Before my last letter to you I had sent you twenty-five liras; you did not mention whether you received it or not after the forty liras. I shall soon send you some more money. The textile business – we shall come to that when this military service issue is settled.

Piraye was here. She stayed a week. Now she has gone back. And my mother will be coming in a day or two. In short, these last two months have gone well.

Please do not neglect writing. Write regularly and consistently, not just at every opportunity, but as much as possible and even at your own personal cost. I miss you very much. For a man in prison, a good friend, a good comrade, an excellent brother and a creative person is half of freedom. I think I have written this to you before; I do not have a single unpleasant memory about you. In my mind you are an unblemished person.

Give me detailed information about how things are with you, and I shall send you some cloth accordingly. As you know, the transfer has to be within a month so that the looms can find the capital. This is the reason I have been hesitant so far. But if your military service is going to be short, I can send you material as soon as you are back. I think this will bring you quite a bit of money through the commission you will get from the sales.

Kiss my daughter and my dearest Yıldız for me. I wish my daughter a comfortable birth and to Yıldız a healthy sibling. I have been shown up as a liar to Yıldız. I bought coffee for her, but was told that the post does not accept monopoly goods, so I could not send it. But I shall certainly send her the toys. Well, farewell for the moment, I am off to the looms. I embrace all of you with longing and affection.

Nâzım

Raşit, my brother,

I received your letter and the magazines. I am writing back immediately.

I sent you the waterproof sheet. Let me know when you receive it. And today I am sending you twenty-five liras. Let me know when you receive that too. Piraye left. My mother arrived. She has also left now. I am alone again. My mother's eyes are getting really clouded over now. She will soon have an operation.[1]

I liked Kadir's[2] poem very much. I am concerned that this good and brave poet will die of malnutrition and neglect, and I am indescribably upset about this. If you know his correct address, I would like to be able to help him if I can. If I can at least send him some money for food. He is a very good poet in every sense of the word.

I shall let you know what I think of your story and Sülker's writings in detail in a day or two.

Yıldız is an amazing girl. She will be a very clever person. Please embrace her and give her lots of kisses for me, but gently, and without hurting her. Your work schedule is excellent, I am very pleased. Don't forget, Raşit, you have to be a world-class writer. In this age of aviation, it is not enough to be a writer on a national scale. I have been rather too involved with the weaving looms, and I have had people coming and going, so I have been neglecting my work, but I have gone back to it today.

I embrace you all with longing. This letter is rather short. The next one will follow tomorrow. I am sending this off immediately so that you will not have to wait for it.

Nâzım

---

1     This is a cataract operation.

2     Abdülkadir Meriçboyu (1917–1985), writer, translator and poet, was one of the young army officers at the Military Academy arrested and tried in early 1938. He spent time in jail with Nâzım and subsequently was exiled to different parts of Anatolia during the forties. In 1967 he published an account of the trial: *1938 Harb Okulu Olayı ve Nâzım Hikmet.*

Raşit,

I am late in answering your letter. We had Republic Day[1] inter-
vening. No one went to the post. I am very glad you have got
a job. Çorbacı is writing you a letter about the silk yarn. Just as
in Europe, I think that once we get over this difficult winter we
shall reach relative prosperity. Once martial law is lifted,[2] we shall
look for a job for you in Istanbul. Who knows, perhaps I may
be out by then.

Kemal Tahir sends you many greetings. I had sent him those
little murmurings of mine, as I sent them to you. He seems to
have liked them very much. I write one such short thing every
evening. Meanwhile I am working on the *Landscapes*.

Let's come to your novel. Start immediately. I really beg you
to do this. If you like, start off with a scaled-down novel first, but
start immediately. START!!!!

You cannot imagine what pleasure it gives me to read what
you write about Nâzım and Yıldız. I am keeping the letters you
send me to provide material for you. It will be of great use to
you one day.

I have not received a letter from Piraye for the last ten days.
I am worried. I shall send a telegram tomorrow. As you know,
the boy's illness has made me totally apprehensive about letters.

Kiss my daughter  for me. I have been neglecting her in
my latest letters. But she should be reassured that she is my
true daughter. That she has given me two grandchildren like
Nâzım and Yıldız is sufficient reason for me to treasure her in
my heart.

---

1    29 October is a national holiday marking the anniversary of the founding
     of the Republic in 1923.
2    Martial law was in force during most of the war years, even though Turkey
     remained neutral until the final stages. It was not lifted until December
     1947.

I think our governor Tahsin Bey[1] is about to resign. It will be a great pity for the prison.

My dear Raşit, most of it is over now. Bear up a little longer. Better days are not far off. I embrace you all with longing, and I look forward to your letters, my dear brother.

Nâzım

Raşit, my brother,

I have received your letter. The order and regularity of your life gives me mounting pleasure. I was upset that you were sacked from your job. What are you going to do now? What happened to the restaurant project? Look, Raşit, you would manage very comfortably if you could engage a little more closely with the sale of our loom products, not just with the profits from your own loom, but also with the commission you will get from the sales of the other looms. I managed to find a little more capital here, and I have extended the business slightly. The yarn business is getting more difficult; I shall have to move over to linen, etc. I am at the experimental stage now. I shall send you samples of our output. If you can find sales outlets for them over there, you will be able to earn more than what you got in the factory when you add the profit of your loom as well. If I send you wide tablecloths in bright colours – the same style as those I sent you previously – how many do you think you will be able to sell? Give me some idea about that so that I can set up the looms accordingly. Those sets do not have buyers here. I shall send you a pair of napkins and a couple of samples of checked cloth in the next post. Make some enquiries about them, and if you manage to get a wholesale order let me know immediately. As for literature:

---

1    Tahsin Akıncı was governor of Bursa Prison 1940–1945. He encouraged artistic activities among the prisoners. His successor also treated Nâzım in a liberal fashion, but a much tougher regime was introduced in the prison in 1948 (Göksu and Timms, 1999, pp. 169–170).

1. Do not neglect French.

2. You are definitely at a point now where you are about to make a break. And this success will have an enormous effect on your future literary activity. I have no doubt that you will be one of the foremost writers of our country... I have often been mistaken in my assessment of people's different attributes. If there is one area, however, where I do not get it wrong, it is assessing people's literary and artistic talent. That is the only area where I have not been duped. In all respects you possess the raw material, the substance and the breath of an artist. I have unbridled confidence in your ability.

My third book has become quite voluminous. I shall send you some passages soon. I am again suffering from sleeplessness. I am losing weight every day. But my enjoyment of life and my hope are intact, as ever.

You hardly mention my daughter and my grandchild in your last letter. But I miss them so very much. Do embrace Yıldız for me; tell her that you are kissing her for her grandpa, and that she should kiss you as if she is kissing me.

It is all as you know here. A piece of news: Kâzım Bey has been released. He cried. Whatever his faults, he was a good man.

Çorbacı, Vasfi and the one from Sarıyer all send lots and lots of greetings. The governor and the registrar also send their greetings.

I shall tell you something which is going to upset and sadden you: my dearest mother, she has cataracts in her eyes. I am so upset about this and probably this is the reason for my lack of sleep. Come, I bid you well, dearest Kemal.

I embrace you all with longing from the depths of my heart.

Nâzım

## 1947

Raşit, I received your New Year wishes, and I wish a very happy new year to you, your wife and my grandchildren. I should be very pleased if you would send me your photograph when you have a new one taken. I could then see how much you have aged, how much more beautiful my daughter has become, and how Yıldız is developing into a splendid young girl and how Nâzım is growing into a young man.

In this envelope I am sending you samples of woollen cloth for women. These are double width, that is 136 centimetres, and there are many other colours. If you can sell these for me at eight liras wholesale, that would be very good. I did a stupid thing and went and borrowed money to get these woven, but, damn this imprisonment, have not been able to sell them. I depend on you, Raşit Efendi.

If you sell them for more than eight liras (the cost to me is eight liras), then I can give you fifty per cent commission. I embrace you, my daughter and my grandchildren with longing.

Nâzım

Raşit, my brother,

Even though my letters have become less frequent, the affection I have for you, my daughter and my grandchildren has not lessened by even a speck. Within my family circle, you are among the first of those I love most. Sometimes I feel the sadness of separation from you very acutely; sometimes I feel the joy of thinking of you all being very happy. Your picture and your photographs are all there at my bedside.

I am as you left me, almost entirely unchanged, or perhaps that is how I feel, but if you saw me perhaps you would find me aged, or on the contrary more youthful.

If you have a group picture taken, send it to me, that will make me very happy. I have a photo of you for almost every year, but I do not have one for this year, 1947.

You must be writing wonderful things. I read a story of yours the other day and was proud of it. I am looking forward to hearing the news of the publication of your novel just as I look forward to a *bayram*.

I clutch you, my daughter and my grandchildren to my bosom, you my most dearly beloved ones.

Nâzım

## 15.2.1949

Raşit, my son,

I received your letter yesterday and am replying at once. You have written wonderful things about me, thank you. I am happier than you can imagine to continue to be so alive in your memories, and to exist there as such a good person. I can assure you that you are similarly alive in my soul, in my heart and in my mind. Your every success in the sphere of arts is to me like a triumph of my own. You are a man worthy of the Turkish people, of honest humanity, of our country and of this beautiful world. As for your novel: I read it all straight through in one sitting as soon as I received it. It brought tears to my eyes. Then, a week later, I read it again, and yet again a third time. It is no mean thing, my dear Raşit's first published novel.[1] Now listen to me: considering that the work will be in four volumes, and that there is only the first volume in hand at the moment, and that like any work of art the novel is also one whole structure, and that

---

1     *Baba Evi* (*My Father's House*), the first of Orhan Kemal's two autobiographical novels. The other is *Avare Yıllar* (*The Idle Years*). An English translation of both novels was published in 2008 as one volume entitled *The Idle Years*. The two novels cover Orhan Kemal's childhood and early adulthood until his marriage.

technical mistakes can occur in the division of the work into different volumes – what a sentence I have structured here, it is like a judicial ruling – yes, without losing sight of any of the things I have just said, listen to me. Firstly, if you ask me, compared to the first two sections, the third section, that is the section about the period after the return to Adana from Syria, that section is rather weak and long. Whereas the lengthy section could better be the section on your father's years in journalism and the party work. In fact, that section is very short, and there are very few characters. I realise that these are only a child's recollections, or rather memories of a childhood, but even so I think it would have been better if that section had been rather more embellished. The part up to there is excellent, superb. Life in Syria is also very real. The characters are very alive – I can almost grab hold of them physically. So I think to combine the first volume with the second volume and – next time, when, one hopes, the second edition appears – to publish it as one book calling this part one and the other part two would be much better. I am content with this section, *My Father's House*, which we shall call part one of the first volume. I love its language. You have now become one of the authors who write Turkish at its best. Good for you. May your hands be blessed. I have not been able to send Kemal's novel back to him. I have been banned from corresponding with him and with political prisoners in general.

I think you must be the only one left who has not heard about this: I have done something totally stupid, something utterly incomprehensible. I decided to divorce Piraye. But I have come to my senses after this seizure of hysteria which has cost me dearly in terms of my health and well-being. I now do not know what to do to get your Yenge to forgive me. Would you ever have guessed that I would do something so stupid? Please do not mention this to my daughter Nuriye; let everyone hear it except her; I should be mortified. I shall write to you at length in one of my future letters about how I got myself into such turmoil, particularly the psychological aspect of it; you are a novelist, you may need it, but at the moment the wound is too fresh, and it has to heal completely before I can delve into what I have gone through and analyse it objectively.

I send my greetings to my daughter over and over again. Just as the greatest fortune and happiness of my life has been to meet a woman like your Piraye Yenge and have her love, friendship, companionship and humanity, your greatest fortune has been to meet my daughter. In the lives of people like you and me the effect of women is something you cannot begin to understand; women play a huge role in our rise and in our fall. You should acknowledge the value and worth of my daughter; your references to her in your letter were full of appreciation and admiration, and this pleased me immensely. I am also glad that you have stopped drinking. You cannot imagine how much I want to see my grandchildren. How strange it is, there are many people I love whose faces I have not seen, whose voices I have not even heard. Some of them were born and brought up without my ever seeing them, and some of them have died.

I am waiting for your photograph with great anticipation – just a snap taken by an amateur or some such, without any touching up. Those are the pictures which are most like one's true self. I shall send you a photograph of me in my next letter. You know (well, how can you know?) my mother has been here for the last month. She comes to visit me every Monday and Thursday. I am so used to it that I do not know what I am going to do when she goes to Adana next month.

I embrace my daughter, my grandchildren and you with longing. Give my respects to your father. Kisses to your mother. Those who got to know you here all send their regards.
Goodbye my dear son.

Nâzım

180

**6.6.1949**

Raşit, my brother,
My delay in replying to you is not in retaliation. It is just that for some time I have been carried away by the prison mood, just sitting around lazily; spring, spring in prison, as you know, I just do not even wish to move.

I am glad that my views about your novel have proved to be correct: that this first book is only one of the volumes, and that it was for technical reasons that they cut it. I mean I am not glad the cuts were made, but that before the cuts the original version was structured more strongly from the technical point of view. However, do not agree to such cuts in the other volumes, and try to have the first volume published once more without the cuts. You cannot imagine with what eager anticipation I await the publication of your other novels, the good news of which you have just given me.

As far as my health is concerned, I manage after a fashion; some itchy blotches which also feel rather hard to the touch have appeared on my face, my nose and my forehead, and they really give me grief.

I loved the idea of Yıldız becoming a dental assistant. While she is getting ready for this she should also continue with her education. When you were her age you were a bit of an idler. But you turned out all right; Yıldız must have taken after you. You must definitely send me a picture of yourselves. The book you say you are planning to write, where you will portray my daughter as the lead character, should be a masterpiece. She is your most precious thing on this earth. How is my namesake? Yıldız has taken after you, but I'd rather she had taken after her mother. I am very

181

sorry about your father's illness. Give him my best wishes for his speedy recovery and my respects. Where we are now is going to become a workplace. Who knows when that will be? If there happens to be a job for me in this workplace then I will both make a living and also fill time; it can also count for exercise.

Well, that is how things are, my dearest brother. I do not even get news of your Yenge. She is furious with me, and she is eighty percent right in that. Over this matter, even I am angry with myself seventy-five percent. Well, goodbye once more. I embrace you, my daughter and the grandchildren with longing, my dear son.

Nâzım

Has been read. 6.6.1949
Acting Governor
Signature


**27.10.1949** (Bursa Prison)

Raşit, my son,
I have received your letter. Before that I received the short story book and the magazines that you sent.[1] I had laid my hands on another issue of that short story magazine. Shall I tell you two things which we should be happy about? Despite some technical shortcomings, almost all the stories in that book were good and promising. Short story writing in Turkey today is in general on the right track. That's one. The second is, of these short stories, the best and the most accomplished – one of them is a little masterpiece – were your stories. May your hands and heart be blessed, Raşit.

As for the photograph, it was a picture taken two or three years ago. I do not know how and where they got it from. In any

---

1    The collection referred to is *Seçilmiş Hikâyeler* (*Selected Short Stories*), which contained short stories by the prominent writers of the time.

case, I am surprised not just at the photograph but at all of the things which have been ascribed to me. Surprise and anger. But whatever: patience and perseverance are needed. As for getting out, I have no hopes. This is also a 'whatever'.

I embrace my grandchildren, my daughter-in-law and you with longing and ask you not to leave me without your letters, my dear brother.

Nâzım

## 6.11.1949

Raşit, my son,
I received your letter and your book.[1] Thank you. Let us talk about the book. Firstly, I did not like the printing. I wish it had been printed on better paper and with a better cover design. But what can we do? We have to be thankful for this much.

I am annoyed with your picture in the book. It is a disgrace. Why did you agree to their printing this? You either put in a picture or you do not, but when you do put one in, then it should be a picture or a photograph that has some artistic value. Whatever.

Let us now come to the work itself. In a word, it is a work worthy of you and the Turkish people, and some stories are masterful, apposite, good and flawless enough to merit a place in world literature. My heart swelled with joy. I became boastful. I finished the book in one night. I noted down some comments underneath the stories. Let me write these down for you.

Yusuf the Infirmary Orderly: 'good'.
Ali the Nightwatchman: 'very good'. The ending is unnecessary.
Page 20: the story should end earlier.

---

1    Orhan Kemal's first book of short stories *Ekmek Kavgası* (*Fight for a Living*).

The Puppy: 'very good'. But this betrays the first signs of a lurking danger.

Bread, Soap and Love: 'very good'.

Around an Orphaned Girl: 'good'.

About a Dead Person: 'good'.

A Human Being: 'good'. It could be shorter.

A Woman: 'very good'.

A New Year Adventure: 'very good'.

The Sleep: 'fantastic'.

The Return: 'that is a little masterpiece'.

About Selling Books: 'very good'. Some endings are constructed with similar elements.

The Propagandist: 'good'.

The Dried-Fruit and Nut Seller: 'good'.

Ali the Child: 'superb'.

Now, my dear Raşit, I shall refer to a couple of technical points. Whether it is in poetry or in prose, sentences structured with the help of commas, semi-colons and even full-stops, that is sentences where the meaning can be confusing if these punctuation marks are missing, are suspect sentences.

Let me give you an example:

'Two hags, behind the regimental kitchen, were sitting across from each other on the damp earth in the field.'

Here the sentence gets its meaning thanks to the comma placed after 'two hags'.[1] If you remove the comma, you get a strange meaning like 'two hags regimental kitchen'. One should structure this sentence as follows:

'On the damp earth in the field behind the regimental kitchen two hags were sitting across from each other.'

---

1    Turkish word order is normally Subject + Object + Verb, and in order to avoid confusion, particularly in long sentences, writers are recommended to put a comma after the subject of the sentence.

I chose this as a random example. Our writers do not pay attention to this at all. I advise you to structure a sentence in such a way that it can be understood clearly without using commas, semi-colons and the like. You can use these as secondary tools, or, if you wish, not at all.

In fact, if the ending of a sentence and the beginning of the next one are only understood through the use of a full-stop, then you must realise that neither sentence has been properly structured. I repeat, sentences that cannot be understood, or can only be understood with difficulty without punctuation marks, are sentences which have been structured wrongly, which have been born dead, structured dead. One should also be very discerning about similes. You sometimes abuse the simile. Two similes in every sentence, or a sequence of similes, are of no use: they will corrupt each other, kill the effect of each other or obscure one another.

Another point:

'The local children who encircled him were naughty and they were fiendish.'

I made this mistake in the past, and to a certain extent deliberately. You should not do it. One should say 'were naughty and fiendish', not *haşindiler*.[1]

After these minor technical matters I move on to the main point.

Today realism is developing in two directions. One direction is the trend which eventually culminates in existentialism, which is reactionary and bereft of hope, with a bleak view of the human race, and is useless and ultimately loses touch with reality. The

---

1   Here the reference is to the use of the third person plural form of the auxiliary verb. The subject of that sentence was in the plural (children), and Nâzım Hikmet is stressing the need to leave the auxiliary in the singular, as the plurality is clear through the use of the plural suffix *-lar* with *çocuk*. This would avoid the unnecessary repetition of the *-lar* suffix in quick succession.

other direction is the trend which unites with a new and creative kind of romanticism; it accepts that the artist is an engineer of the psyche, and because of that in the end it represents reality best. Some of your short stories are not just sad, they are touched by hopelessness. In recent years, for obvious reasons, this tendency is on the increase, particularly in our short story writers. Reality, essentially through its own historic course, is not hopeless. It has its sad, anguished, bitter, twilight, abhorrent, abominable, contemptible, vile aspects. The slightest negligence in conveying these aspects results in representing humanity without impartiality and through rose-tinted spectacles, and it means moving away from reality. But despite all this, through the work of man, this reality is developing and moving towards the better and the more pleasing. What is developing is not without hope, it is not without joy. I am emphasising this point because whether an individual is in the grip of hope or hopelessness is a matter which concerns only that individual. But, for instance, just as a doctor who believes that men's fight against disease is in vain should have no right to practise as a doctor, similarly a writer who offers no hope has no right to be a writer. No one can take away this right from such writers by force, but ultimately reality obliterates them. Great writers like Shakespeare, Cervantes, Balzac, Tolstoy, Chekhov and Gorky are at times horrifically sad, bitter, despondent authors, but they are always hopeful. Think of the play *Hamlet*. Think of *Don Quixote*. Think of *War and Peace* and *My Universities*. On the other hand, Dostoyevsky, who is on a par with them individually, will ultimately fade away. There are reasons to be sad, disconsolate, bitter, but there is not a single reason to be hopeless.

Beware, my son, protect yourself from this, be even more bitter and sad, but let your joy and hope shine through. That's it. I repeat once more, I congratulate you and Turkish Literature. Young and old, I clutch you all to my bosom.

Nâzım

# NAMES, TITLES AND MODES
# OF ADDRESS

⚒

Until the twentieth century, surnames or family names were not generally used in Turkey (with exceptions among some well-todo families and members of certain tribes). The father's name would normally follow the given name. In 1934, however, as part of the Republican reforms, a law was passed requiring all citizens to choose a surname. The names of Atatürk and İnönü were bestowed by the Turkish Grand National Assembly on Mustafa Kemal Paşa and İsmet Paşa respectively. Later that year another law formally abolished a number of traditional Ottoman titles.

In formal contexts, Turks today are addressed as *Sayın* (applicable to both sexes) with the surname, or as *Bay* (for men) and *Bayan* (for women).

In less formal contexts, but to show respect, it is more usual to use the titles *Bey* and *Hanım*, roughly equivalent to 'Mr' and 'Mrs', except that they are placed after the first name. Orhan Kemal refers to Emin Bey with this title to denote respect, probably because he was older than the others, like İzzet and Necati. The title was originally used to designate a gentleman or nobleman, or person of standing. Orhan Kemal uses it somewhat sarcastically to describe the Azerbaijani prisoner, and in this context it has been translated here as 'gent'. *Bey* and *Hanım* are also used in the plural to mean 'gentlemen' and 'ladies' respectively.

*Bey* and *Hanım* were among those titles formally abolished in 1934, but they are nevertheless still widely used in non-official contexts. Two other modes of address which appear in this book were also on the list of abolished titles but are still used unofficially:

*Efendi*, following the first name, was used for Ottoman Princes and notables, but in Republican times has been used to address or refer to men who are considered of lower social rank than those addressed as *Bey*. It is now obsolescent in this sense.

*Paşa* was the official title of a general, admiral or senior civil official. It is now used informally to refer to generals and admirals, who are often addressed in the possessive form *Paşam* ('my Paşa').

Turks feel uneasy addressing someone by their first name alone, even when they are quite close, and throughout the book people are addressed by a range of expressions indicating respect, depending on the relative social status of the speakers.

Nâzım Hikmet in particular is addressed as *üstat*, which has been translated as 'master'. It is used throughout the book as an honorific and as a means of address to denote respect. It suggests that Orhan Kemal and others regard Nâzım Hikmet as the practitioner *par excellence* of the art of poetry. It also carries something of the connotation of 'hero'.

*Usta*, which in modern Turkish is a different word, designates a skilled craftsman. Galip Usta is the character in the opening lines of Nâzım Hikmet's *Human Landscapes from my Country* who is standing on the station steps.

It is also usual to address people, or to refer to them, with designations of kinship, even when there is no actual family relationship between the people concerned. A number of these have been retained in Turkish in the translation:

*Abi*, sometimes spelt *Ağabey* – Orhan Kemal uses both spellings – means 'elder brother', but is used to address men who may or may not be older than the speaker to denote both closeness and respect. It is used both alone and following the first name. The gypsy who tells Nâzım Hikmet that someone has tried to take out a contract on him addresses him repeatedly as *Abi* to ingratiate himself with the poet.

*Yenge* means 'a man's brother's wife'. It is a less formal means of addressing a woman than *Hanım,* even outside the context of kinship. It is used by men in addressing women in the presence of their husbands to indicate closeness as well as respect – thus Orhan Kemal and the other prisoners refer to Nâzım Hikmet's wife Piraye as Piraye *Yenge* or just as *Yenge.*

*Baba* means 'father'. It is used informally to address or refer to an older man, either by itself or following the first name.

*Dede* means 'grandfather'. Like *Baba* it is used informally to address or refer to an older man, either by itself or following the first name, but it designates someone who is really old.

*Kadın* means 'woman', but here corresponds to an informal equivalent of 'Mrs'. It indicates a person of humble social origins. It is not very usual today to refer to someone as Fatma Kadın. For Nâzım she represents a simple village woman, a figure to be found all over Turkey. Fatma is one of the most common names, particularly among rural people. Nâzım's mother, an Istanbul lady, would be addressed as Celile Hanım, not as Celile Kadın.

Like many European languages, the second person plural *siz* ('you') is used in Turkish to show respect, with the familiar singular *sen* form (literally 'thou', like the French *tu*) being used between close friends, colleagues and the like. Orhan Kemal writes that he and Nâzım were addressing each other with the informal *sen*. He uses the Turkish word *senlibenli* to explain this, when he is expressing his amazement at how quickly he came to be chatting easily to the poet he had admired for so long. Throughout the book, however, the conversations between the two men as he records them are conducted using the formal plural *siz*, corresponding to the French *vous*.

# BIBLIOGRAPHY

※

Aykut, Ebru, 'Constructing Divisions Between City and Countryside in *On Fertile Lands* and *Distant'*, *Journal of Historical Studies,* 5 (2007, pp. 69–82).

Balaban, İbrahim, *Şair Baba ve Damdakiler* (İstanbul: Cem Yayınevi, 1968).

Bezirci, Asım and Altınkaynak, Hikmet, *Orhan Kemal* (İstanbul: Cem Yayınevi, 1977).

Çelik, Zeynep, *The Remaking of Istanbul* (Berkeley: University of California Press, 1986).

Demirel, Merâl, *Tam Bir Muhalif Abdülkadir Kemali Bey* (İstanbul: İstanbul Bilgi Üniversitesi Yayınları, 2006).

Göksu, Saime and Timms, Edward, *Romantic Communist: The Life and Work of Nâzım Hikmet* (London: Hurst and Company, 1999).

Gönenç, Turgay, 'Yazarlıktaki ilk öğretmenim Orhan Kemal' (*Cumhuriyet Kitap*, 10 Nisan 2008).

Gültekin, M. Nuri, *Orhan Kemal'in Romanlarında Modernleşme Birey ve Gündelik Hayat* (Ankara: Ürün Yayınları, 2007).

Hale, William, *Turkish Foreign Policy 1774–2000* (London and Portland: Frank Cass, 2000). 214

Harris, George, *The Origins of Communism in Turkey* (Stanford: Hoover Institution Publications, 1967).

Hikmet, Nâzım, *Bütün Şiirleri* (Istanbul: Yapı Kredi Yayınları 2476, 4. baskı 2008).

Hikmet, Nâzım, ed. Tahir, Kemal, *Kemal Tahir'e Mahpushaneden Mektuplar* (İstanbul: Bilgi Yayınları, 1968).

Hikmet, Nâzım, ed. Va-Nu, Müzehher, *Bursa Cezaevinden Va-Nu'lara Mektuplar* (İstanbul: Cem Yayınevi, 1970).

Hikmet, Nâzım, *Human Landscapes from my Country*, tr. Randy Blasing and Mutlu Konuk (New York: Persea, 2002).

Kadir, A. (Abdülkadir Meriçboyu), *1938 Harb Okulu Olayı ve Nâzım Hikmet* (İstanbul: İstanbul Matbaası, 1967).

Kemal, Orhan, *72. Koğuş* (İstanbul: Everest, 2007).

Kemal, Orhan, *The Prisoners*, translation of *72. Koğuş* by Cengiz Lugal (İstanbul: Anatolia Publishing).

Kemal, Orhan, *Baba Evi* (İstanbul: Varlık Yayınları, 1949).

Kemal, Orhan, *Avare Yıllar* (İstanbul: Varlık Yayınları, 1950).

Kemal, Orhan, *The Idle Years*, translation of *Baba Evi* and *Avare Yıllar* by Cengiz Lugal (London and Chester Springs: Peter Owen, 2008).

Kemal, Orhan, *Bereketli Topraklar Üzerinde* (İstanbul: Epsilon, 2007).

Kemal, Orhan, *Bir Filiz Vardı* (İstanbul: Epsilon, 2006).

Kemal, Orhan, *Cemile* (İstanbul: Varlık Yayınları, 1952).

Kemal, Orhan, *Gemilé*, translation of *Cemile* by Cengiz Lugal (İstanbul: Anatolia Publishing).

Kemal, Orhan, *Ekmek Kavgası (Fight for a Living)* (İstanbul: Varlık Yayınları, 1950).

Kemal, Orhan, *Grev* (Ankara: Seçilmiş Hikâyeler Dergisi Kitapları, 1954).

Kemal, Orhan, *Hanımın Çiftliği* (İstanbul: Everest, 2008).

Kemal, Orhan, *Kardeş Payı* (Epsilon, 2006).

Kemal, Orhan, *Murtaza* (İstanbul: Varlık Yayınları, 1952).

Kemal, Orhan, *Nâzım Hikmetle 3,5 Yıl* (İstanbul: Sosyal Yayınlar, 1965).

Kemal, Orhan, ed. Öğütçü, Işık, *Önemli Not! Tamamlanmamış Yapıtlar ve Seçilmiş Düzyazılar* (İstanbul: Everest, 2007).

Kemal, Orhan, *Sokaklardan Bir Kız* (İstanbul: Epsilon 2005).

Kemal, Orhan, *Suçlu* (İstanbul: Everest, 2008).

Kudret, Cevdet, *Türk Edebiyatında Hikaye ve Roman* (Ankara: İnkilap Yayınları, 1999).

Kurdakul, Şükran, *Çağdaş Türk Edebiyatı 4* (Ankara: Bilgi Yayınevi, 1992).

Mango, Andrew, *Atatürk* (London: John Murray, 1999).

Moran, Berna, *Türk Romanına Eleştirel Bir Bakış II* (İstanbul: İletişim Yayınları, 1990).

Naci, Fethi, *Elli Türk Romanı* (İstanbul: Oğlak Yayıncılık, 1997).

Öğütçü, Işık, ed., *Orhan Kemal'ın Babası Abdülkadir Kemali'nin Anıları* (İstanbul: Epsilon, 2005).

Pierce, Joe E., *Life in a Turkish Village* (New York: Holt, Rinehart and Winston, 1965).

Rathbun, Carole, *The Village in the Turkish Novel and Short Story 1920–1955* (The Hague: Mouton, 1972).

Stirling, Paul, *Turkish Village* (London: Weidenfeld and Nicolson, 1965).

Taner, Haldun, *Ölürse Ten Ölür Canlar Ölesi Değil* (Ankara: Bilgi Yayınevi, 1986).

Uğurlu, Nurer, *Orhan Kemal'in İkbal Kahvesi* (İstanbul: Örgün Yayınevi, 2002).

Ünlü, Mahir, and Özcan, Ömer, *Yirminci Yüzyıl Türk Edebiyatı* (İstanbul: İnkılap Kitabevi, 1991)